Gear-Shifting Leadership

Gear-Shifting Leadership

A Manager's Guide for Developing Effective Leaders

Second Edition

Leon Cai

Routledge
Taylor & Francis Group

A PRODUCTIVITY PRESS BOOK

First published 2021
by Routledge
600 Broken Sound Parkway #300, Boca Raton FL, 33487

and by Routledge
2 Park Square, Milton Park, Abingdon, Oxon OX14 4RN

Routledge is an imprint of the Taylor & Francis Group, an informa business

© 2021 Taylor & Francis

Library of Congress Cataloging-in-Publication Data
A catalog record for this title has been requested

ISBN: 978-0-367-82032-9 (hbk)
ISBN: 978-0-367-80278-3 (pbk)
ISBN: 978-1-00-301153-8 (ebk)

Typeset in Minion
by Newgen Publishing UK

Contents

PART IV   Organizational Executive Leadership

About the Author

 **Leon Cai** is a global partner of Perth Leadership Institute and represents Perth in Shanghai, China. He is also the Dean as well as Chief Consultant of Wilner Sales & Leadership Institute. Leon was once ranked among the top ten most influential Chinese trainers and was the winner of the "Honor China Award". He was recommended by the Discovery Channel of CCTV (Central TV station of China) as a leading figure in China's training and consulting industry.

Leon Cai graduated from Fudan University, a top-level university in China. He had been a management consultant in a renowned consulting firm and a senior marketing director in a fortune 500 company before starting his career as a trainer, speaker and writer. He was certified as "writer of the year" by Enterprise Management Publishing house as well as China Fortune Press.

Leon Cai is the author of many bestsellers in China. Besides *Gear-shifting Leadership,* he has also published *Key Controlling Points of Sales Management; Soft Negotiation; Blue Marketing, Red Sales; Left-Hand Service, Right-Hand Sales;* and *Strategic Selling.*

Preface

Over the past 20 years, I was quite lucky to be offered various opportunities of being trained and coached by a dozen international experts who were renowned in the field of leadership development. What impressed me strongly was that leadership models of these experts differed from each other greatly in terms of objective, perspective, process and effect.

My interest in finding the linkage between varieties of leadership models was generated due to the motivation and encouragement from some of these experts. Then my work aimed at integrating different components of leadership in a new framework which continued for three years until the mode of gear-shifting leadership was successfully developed.

The first edition of *Gear-Shifting Leadership* was published in 2012 in Chinese. It won high praise and great recognition from the business as well as academic circle of China. Since then I have been busy delivering leadership training and offering consulting services to many enterprises and other types of organizations in China and some other Asian countries. As there are increasing numbers of English-speaking audiences and readers, I felt it vital to update my book with better examples as well as additional tools and have its English edition published.

I sincerely hope this English edition can also win recognition from readers of Western countries and the framework of gear-shifting can help deepen their understanding of leadership from a new perspective. Any helpful suggestions, advice or criticisms from readers in different countries will be most welcome.

I should express my sincere gratitude to Cris Yu, my wife; Sunny Huang, my elder daughter; and Miko Yu, my younger daughter for their understanding and support.

Leon Cai

Introduction—Four Gears of Leadership Development

MID- AND HIGH-LEVEL MANAGERS NEED MORE COMPREHENSIVE LEADERSHIP

In the past decades, theories, schools of thought and methodologies related to or named after leadership have emerged endlessly. Under the label of *leadership*, a number of aspects representing different perspectives have been studied: communication-oriented, controlling-oriented, coaching-oriented, change-oriented, psychology-oriented, team development-oriented and organizational behavior-oriented.

Yet sadly, these modes focusing on one or several certain aspects of leadership tend to be mistaken as the panorama or general landscape of leadership. We see in practice that it is difficult for leaders to resolve complicated management issues and deal with ever-changing leadership challenges through the employment of such incomplete models. We may often run into the following incomprehensible phenomena in management practices:

- Why can't a charismatic leader with excellent self-management skills build an excellent team?
- Why can't a leader skilled in coaching team members adapt himself or herself to a revolutionary or innovative management environment?
- Why can't a leader good at strategic planning cultivate core backbones capable of sharing his or her own duties?
- Why can't a leader with outstanding team management ability be recognized and supported by his or her superiors?
- Why will prominent mid-level or grassroots managers perform poorly in terms of leadership once they are promoted to higher positions?

All of these seemingly incomprehensible phenomena actually illustrate that these leaders are only excellent in one certain aspect of leadership. In other words, leaders' skill improvement in a certain aspect of leadership doesn't necessarily mean their complete upgrade of overall leadership ability.

Mid- and high-level managers of any type of organizations are faced with much more leadership challenges than grassroots businesses. They need to manage both direct subordinates and indirect subordinates. They are responsible not only for managing staff and teams but also for formulating mechanisms and systems. They should pay attention to both the achievement of short-term objectives and the realization of long-term organizational strategies. They have to balance the partial interests of their own teams and the overall interests of the whole organization.

As a result, mid- and high-level managers need to master not just one or several aspects of leadership but a complete leadership system. Take driving a car for example, drivers should keep switching the gears of their cars in the driving process so as to ensure the smooth movement of their cars under any circumstances.

The gears of any kind of vehicles are composed of many interlinked parts. If leadership is compared to the gears of vehicles, the same principle applies. Different components (aspects) of leadership, which are like the numerous parts in the gears, are by no means arranged together in a disorderly way. On the contrary, various aspects of leadership should be integrated structurally into several leadership gears.

It is the basic mechanism of gear-shifting in cars that gear-shifting leadership refers to. Varieties of leadership aspects are grouped into four gears and the whole leadership system is comprised of these four gears.

FOUR GEARS OF LEADERSHIP DEVELOPMENT

Gear-shifting leadership got its name from the analogy to a core component of automobiles—the gear. Leaders need to greatly improve and perfect their own leadership gears in order to develop their teams, control their organizations and cope with changes. Comprehensive leadership is formed through the mutual interaction and perfect combination of four gears.

The four gears of leadership are defined respectively as *followership, face-to-face leadership, indirect leadership* and *organizational executive leadership*. All of them are indispensable to the effectiveness of leadership as a whole.

- Followership is the basis where leaders can exhibit their personal charisma and obtain trust and recognition from others. Specifically, followership includes two dimensions of trust-winning. Leaders win trust from their subordinates through exemplary self-management and obtain trust from their superiors through superb upward management.
- Face-to-face leadership reflects leaders' ability to motivate, inspire, instruct, control and develop direct subordinates and core teams. It shows leaders' one-on-one leadership abilities targeted at developing capable and conscientious direct subordinates.
- Indirect leadership refers to leaders' influences and driving powers on indirect subordinates and their teams as a whole. It focuses on the overall performances of teams rather than performances of subordinates as individuals. It can be defined as leaders' one-to-many abilities targeted at developing high-performance teams.
- Organizational executive leadership shows leaders' keen observation toward dynamic changes inside and outside their organizations. It defines a leader's abilities to dynamically adjust their management modes and leadership styles in order to adapt to the internal and external organizational changes.

In short, followership is leaders' ability to lead themselves, face-to-face leadership is their ability to lead individuals, indirect leadership defines their ability to lead teams and organizational executive leadership refers to their ability to lead organizations (i.e., leading from the perspective of organizational changes).

Four Gears of Leadership Development

Four Leadership Gears	Definition and Characteristics	Object of Leadership
GEAR1 Followership	Followership is the basis on which leaders exhibit their own charisma and obtain others' trust.	Leaders themselves

Four Leadership Gears	Definition and Characteristics	Object of Leadership
	Leaders win trust from subordinates through exemplary self-management and obtain support from superiors through excellent upward management.	
GEAR2 Face-to-face Leadership	Face-to-face leadership shows the leader's ability to motivate, encourage, instruct, control and develop direct subordinates and core teams. It defines the leader's one-on-one leadership ability aimed at developing capable and responsible direct subordinates.	Direct subordinates as individuals
GEAR3 Indirect Leadership	Indirect leadership refers to leaders' influences and driving forces on indirect subordinates and their team as a whole. When the number of direct subordinates far exceeds the optimum span of management, leaders should shift their gears from face-to-face leadership to indirect leadership.	Teams as a whole
GEAR4 Organizational Executive Leadership	Organizational executive leadership demonstrates leaders' keen observation and overall view on the dynamic changes in their organizations. It defines leaders' abilities to adjust and optimize their own management modes and leadership styles in order to adapt to internal and external changes.	Organizations

FIGURE I.1
Four leadership gears.

All four gears are indispensable components of gear-shifting leadership. They interact with each other and work together in combination. Should there be faults or problems in any one of the four gears, there may be severe damage or collapse to leaders' comprehensive leadership no matter how excellent their performances are in other gears (Figure I.1).

For example, there are some leaders who attach little importance to the development of followership. They fail to practice what they preach and cannot set good examples to others. No matter how excellent their performance is in other gears, they will finally lose trust from subordinates, superiors and others. The other three gears will lose effect due to the lack of trust.

In other situations, if some managers are not good at organizational executive leadership, there will be inconsistencies and conflicts between their own management method and the overall strategic development of their organization—no matter how well they perform other three gears.

There are also some managers who are unable to shift from face-to-face leadership to indirect leadership. They can be outstanding leaders of small teams but may encounter lots of challenges while managing large-scale teams with a complicated organizational hierarchy.

Part I

Followership

1

Followers and Leaders

WHY SHOULD LEADERS DEVELOP FOLLOWERSHIP?

The maxim of soldiers who do not want to be marshals are not good soldiers has inspired many young men who are aspiring to be leaders. However, a more reflective question derived from this maxim is whether a marshal who cannot even be a good soldier is a good marshal.

A young candidate came across a question while filling in an application form for the position of management trainee in a well-known multinational enterprise. The question was: "Did you used to be a good leader?" After thinking for a while, he finally decided to write down these words truthfully: "No, I used to be a good employee." When he submitted the application form, he was sure that the answer had deprived him of this opportunity.

But before long, he received a phone call from the HR director of the company.

Until today, we have received thousands of application forms. Almost all of the applicants wrote down in the application letters that they used to be good leaders. You are the only one who answered no. Our boss decided to meet you in person for a face-to-face talk. Although we are recruiting a management trainee who is the future manager of our company, we firmly believe that a good manager should undoubtedly be a good subordinate first. More importantly, we have discovered an excellent character in you which is indispensable both to employees and to managers, that is honesty,

said the HR director over the phone. This simple case illustrates the relationship between leadership and followership. One who cannot even be a good soldier can never develop into an excellent marshal. Likewise, one who doesn't have the excellent characters of employees cannot become a truly extraordinary leader. Any leader who expects to be more excellent, outstanding and influential than others, must learn how to be an excellent follower first. Leaders should base the development of leadership on how they shape followership.

For any type of leader, the first and foremost goal of self-cultivation is not to study how to improve leadership but to learn how to become qualified followers. Many managers may take it for granted that what they need to improve should be focused on how to lead others and how to make further breakthroughs in their leadership. They do not believe there is still a need to develop their followership ability because they don't understand the three positive effects followership has on the improvement of leadership. Integration of dual roles, combination of dual behaviors and development of similar characters are the three positive effects of followership that leaders should be clear about, which are listed in Table 1.1.

TABLE 1.1

Three Positive Effects of Followership on the Improvement of Leadership

Integration of Dual Roles	• In any organization or team, the majority of managers have dual identities and roles. As the leaders of their subordinates they have the responsibility of downward management. Meanwhile, they are also the followers of their superiors with upward management being an indispensable part of their responsibilities. • By learning and developing followership, leaders are enabled to think and act from the perspective of both followership and leadership.
Combination of Dual Behaviors	• Both followership and leadership are important tools for influencing and managing others, which leaders can use situationally by leaders. Leadership and followership behaviors can be selectively adapted to different subordinates. • Managers can treat some subordinates with particular experiences, skills, resources or backgrounds as special superiors and adopt followership behaviors instead of leadership behaviors toward them. • Numerous cases show that leaders who play the role of followers toward some select superiors will gain much more recognition, trust and support from their team members.
Development of Similar Characteristics	• Although positions or job requirements of followers and leaders may differ from each other, the qualities and characteristics required for both are similar. • Leaders who become skilled with the followership technique will become adept at winning trust more so than other leaders.

THE BASIC DEFINITION AND CONNOTATION OF FOLLOWERSHIP

Follower refers to a person who follows others' opinions and instructions or obeys others' orders. Followers are not always those who are at lower organizational levels. Subordinates can be leaders and their superiors can also be followers. For example, a new general manager of a manufacturing department often asked for advice and suggestions in a non-assuming way from a senior engineer who had over 20 years of work experience. He not only kept nodding while listening but also praised the engineer all the time. What's more, he provided prompt feedback to the engineer for each of his suggestions. Obviously, the new general manager played the role of follower in front of the experienced engineer and treated him as his superior in this scenario.

There is one definition and two cores of followership shown in Table 1.2 for a leader's comprehensive understanding of the technique.

Leaders should understand that the relationship between leadership and followership is not static but dynamic and changeable. More specifically:

- The roles of followers and leaders are relative and in constant change. In different periods, different occasions and different organizations, leaders can become followers and vice versa.

TABLE 1.2

One Definition and Two Cores of Followership

One Definition of Followership	Leaders with excellent followership abilities can win consistent trust and universal recognition from both superiors and subordinates.	
Two Cores of Followership	1. Self-management	Leaders need to practice what they preach and show a high level of self-discipline. They should be capable of setting good examples and being excellent models to others and gain trust from subordinates.
	2. Upward management	Leaders need to build mutual trust with their superiors and obtain support from the top by practicing upward management. Superiors referred to here can include leaders supervisors, peers and even experienced subordinates.

- Followers and leaders are mutually following and mutually leading. Leaders can choose followers and followers can also choose leaders. If followers are dissatisfied with their leaders, they can also stop following and cease their relationships.

INTERACTION BETWEEN FOLLOWERS AND LEADERS

Allen, the creative director of a well-known PR company, recently recruited four college graduates through campus recruitment. According to the suggestion from Jason, CEO of the company, the purpose of recruitment was to supplement fresh blood and increase the vitality and creativity in his department.

One month later, Jason asked Allen over dinner about the performance of the four newcomers. Allen heaved a long sigh and said that "The differences between the four could never be recognized during the interview. But in no more than three months, their differences are very obvious."

Jason's interest was aroused, "Why do you say that?"

Allen said,

Take Andy who graduated from a well-known university for example. He is indeed a capable person with unique and creative ideas, but we always feel that he is not an active participant in team activities. He seldom speaks during team brainstorming sessions and is unwilling to join any group discussions. Besides, he often disagrees with the determined decisions of our team. I used to invite him for coffee and chat with him in an informal way, but he always seemed very sensitive and kept a certain psychological distance from me. His abilities have been tested and proved during the past three months, but he is still unwilling to integrate himself into our team.

While Benson, who was strongly recommended by one of our clients, can't be relied on for important projects or urgent tasks. He doesn't have enough ability to complete assignments independently and mistakes were often made if I did not follow up closely. What's more, he is not enthusiastic and passionate in his daily work.

Cindy, who used to be an intern here, has a close interpersonal relationship me. She always asks me about anything that is unclear to her and will spare no effort to do what is assigned to her. But until now she still cannot complete tasks without my coaching, instructions, and support.

Duncan has become the most satisfying staff member on my team. Although not competitive in terms of educational background, he has strong self-learning abilities and keeps sharpening his professional skills. In addition, he is so proactive at work that he often asks for more assignments after accomplishing his own. I rarely have to worry about the tasks handed over to him as he always delivers the desired outcome.

"Yes, those four new staff are quite different from each other because they are different types of followers," Jason commented. Allen's remarks were made about his own day-to-day perspective, while Jason summarized by differentiating them in terms of type of follower. Followers can be categorized into four types by two dimensions which are *attitude* and *ability*. The level of attitude can be examined by *active* or *inactive* and the level of ability can be appraised by *dependent* or *independent*.

Independent followers are capable of completing tasks and achieving goals without others' support or help. What's more, these followers are also independent thinkers and will not lean too much on their leaders. On the contrary, dependent followers are incapable of completing tasks and achieving goals on their own. Active followers are those who are proactive, enthusiastic and self-motivated.

In Figure 1.1, note that followers who are active but dependent are categorized into the submissive type, followers who are inactive and

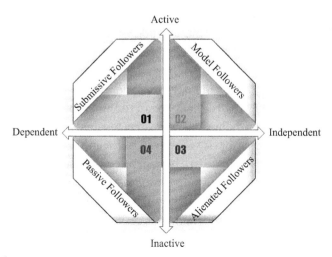

FIGURE 1.1
Four types of followers.

dependent are classified into the passive type, followers who are independent but inactive are categorized into the alienated type and followers who are active and independent are classified into the model type. Different types of followers have different behavioral characteristics, which is shown in Table 1.3.

Obviously, the four college graduates in Allen's case belonged to different types of followers. Andy was an alienated follower, Benson was a passive follower, Cindy was a submissive follower, and Duncan was a model follower.

Roger was a mid-level manager in a large manufacturing enterprise, responsible for a department comprised of 18 employees. Roger was active in giving every subordinate care and consideration and was on good terms with his team members. However, he was too dependent on Jack, the vice president of his company. No matter what was assigned by Jack, Roger would immediately require his subordinates to do without questioning. Once subordinates raised different opinions on the decisions made by Jack, he would always say, "Now that Jack has decided, we shall execute with no excuse. He is our leader, so we should do whatever our leader asks us to do."

In the beginning, Roger's subordinates understood his behavior and followed his instructions to a T, but gradually they no longer asked Roger for help when there was confusion or an unseen challenge. Instead, they would directly ask for instructions from Jack without informing Roger because most of them lost trust in Roger's abilities as a qualified leader. Over time, Roger found that the attitude of the team toward him had changed greatly. They no longer respected him as before. What's more, some even openly opposed his opinions and refused to execute the tasks assigned by him. Finally, his inability was widely recognized by everyone on his team and all the subordinates began to think nothing of him.

In this case, Roger's failure as a leader resulted from his excessive dependence on his superior. It was obviously seen that Roger was a submissive follower with a high degree of dependence on his superior and low degree of activeness in his working attitude. Leaders who are submissive followers of their superiors will possibly lose the respect and trust from their subordinates as it was shown in this case.

Additionally, the followership type of Roger's subordinates also underwent a process of conversion and change. In the beginning, the 18 subordinates would carefully execute Roger's orders and they could be

TABLE 1.3

Behavioral Characteristics of Four Types of Followers

Submissive Followers	• Submissive followers are willing to follow instructions and obey orders from leaders. They never complain and always actively execute what is assigned to them. These followers are excessively active and have a strong allegiance to their managers, it may be quite dangerous if the mission they execute conflicts with the regulations or policies of the organization.
	• Submissive followers are active participants in team activities. They regard themselves as indispensable contributors to team performance. But they place excessive trust on their leaders and lack enough ability to work or think on their own.
	• Submissive followers are in urgent need of upgrading working capabilities and professional skills so as to lessen their reliance on leaders.
Passive Followers	• Passive followers will not act without orders or commands from their leaders. Without the encouragement and supervision from others, they will never take initiative in executing a certain task. As they are not proactive and lack a sense of duty, passive followers will not do anything until they receive guidance or instructions from leaders.
	• Many leaders believe that followers of this type are deeply influenced and determined by their personalities. In the eyes of their leaders, passive followers are introverted, characterless, lazy and incapable.
	• Passive followers are not strong-minded and prefer to follow the crowd. They need to improve their ability to think on their own and act accordingly.
Alienated Followers	• Alienated followers always keep a certain distance from leaders and remain both independent and inactive. They tend to feel good about themselves and believe in their ability to handle problems well. Therefore, they are not dependent on nor do they rely on their leaders. On the contrary, they often disagree with the decisions made by their leaders and disobey the regulations of their teams.
	• Alienated followers think independently and maintain their own perspectives. They are used to criticizing and repudiating leaders' decisions and behaviors. They always express different opinions and put forward different proposals.
Model Followers	• Followers of model type not only keep pace with their leaders but also think and act independently. They will propose constructive suggestions to leaders actively.
	• When their personal viewpoints differ from decisions made by their leaders, model followers will still respect, accept and execute the tasks that are assigned to them.
	• Model followers always act as the leader's spokesperson, promoting the leaders' influence and reputation inside their teams.

considered as submissive or model followers. But with their increasing distrust toward Roger and their recognition of his inability, they gradually turned into alienated or passive followers.

From Roger's case, we see a dynamic process of mutual interaction between leaders and followers. What's more, the followership type of leaders will gradually influence and change the followership type of their subordinates. Roger's behavior as a submissive follower are closely related to the management and leadership style of his supervisor, Jack.

If Jack, as his leader, found out the dramatic change in the follower type of Roger's subordinates, an intervention should have been conducted to give Roger enough authorization and coaching not to change that team's dynamic. He should try to develop Roger into a model follower by nurturing independent thinking and working ability.

Suppose that Roger deeply realized his own problems and had a strong willingness to improve, he should actively shape himself into a model follower. Once Roger became a model follower, the followership type of his team would also change. Some subordinates who restored their confidence in the working ability of Roger would possibly become submissive followers again. A few subordinates could even develop into model followers (Figure 1.2).

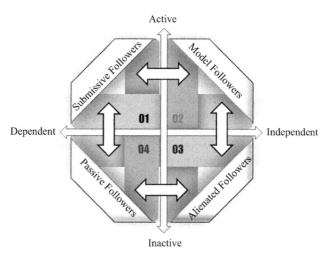

FIGURE 1.2
Transformation between different types of followers.

For managers at various organizational levels who are both leaders and followers, the four types of followership and the relationship between these roles can help in improvement in the following ways:

- Leaders should diagnose their own type of followership and analyze whether their approach can help them build harmonious relationships and mutual trust with their superiors. Leaders should convert themselves into and act as model followers in the eyes of their superiors.
- Leaders should analyze the followership types of their team members and evaluate the proportion of the various types. Leaders need to increase the number of model followers and reduce the proportion of alienated followers by changing their own way of management and leadership.
- Leaders should identify whether there are some subordinates with special expertise, experiences and resources in some areas and treat them as special superiors. For these subordinates, it is better for leaders to adopt behaviors of followership rather than to win recognition and support from them.

2

Two Cores of Followership

The fundamental objective of followership development is to improve the leader's abilities for winning others' trust, recognition and support. For leaders at various organizational levels, the most critical trust and support that they hope to obtain typically comes from two areas, namely, subordinates and superiors. Trust from subordinates can greatly improve the effective implementation of the mission and tasks assigned by leaders, while trust from superiors enable leaders to obtain more support, resource and help from the top.

In order to win trust from both subordinates and superiors, leaders need to develop two types of followership styles: self-management and upward management. Obviously, strict self-management can help leaders win authentic recognition and respect from subordinates, while superb upward management enables leaders to earn the support of their superiors.

Self-management and upward management are inseparable and interconnected—both are indispensable components of followership. Leaders who do not excel at upward management may find it difficult to gain praise and recognition from their superiors no matter how outstanding their self-management is. What's more, these leaders may find that they cannot obtain enough resources and support from the top.

On the contrary, leaders who are skillful at upward management but poor in self-management always find that subordinates' willingness and motivation to execute on a mission are low due to their lack of trust toward them. What's more, the recognition from superiors will also decline gradually as superiors' dissatisfaction with the leader's poor downward management increases (Figure 2.1).

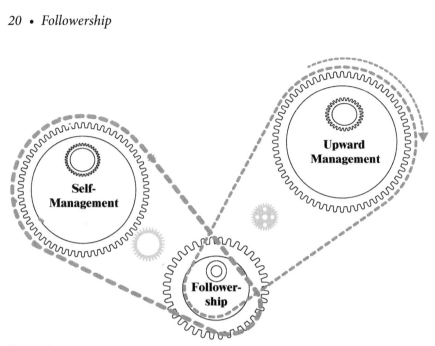

FIGURE 2.1
Two cores of followership.

5Q MODEL OF LEADERS' SELF-MANAGEMENT

Liu Chuanzhi, former chairman of the board of directors of Lenovo, is an outstanding entrepreneur and widely recognized as the godfather of management in China. Once a journalist interviewed him and asked, "Many people are attracted by your personal charisma and admire you for it, what is the greatest merit of your personality?" Liu Chuanzhi answered, "Self-discipline." The greatness of a person lies in managing himself or herself instead of leading others, Liu Chuanzhi emphasized repeatedly.

Excellent leaders do not threaten and force others to do what they are unwilling to do by their position of power. Instead, they always win compliance and support from employees by their personal charisma and character. Subordinates evaluate leaders more on their character than on their knowledge. Subordinates appraise leaders more by their behavior than by their intelligence. Subordinates base their assessment of leaders more on what they have done than what they have said.

We can always find inconsistencies of some leaders between their words and deeds. For example, some leaders declare on various occasions that they attach great importance to the benefits of employees and they are people-oriented. But in reality, what they do is completely opposite from what they say. They are unwilling to listen to the complaints of employees and are indifferent to the real needs of their employees. They may let excellent employees leave without making any effort to retain them.

In fact, employees feel it impossible to trust leaders who fail to manage themselves. Their dissatisfaction toward such unqualified leaders will finally lead to complete loss of their trust for the entire team as well as organization. In other words, leaders' poor self-management will lower subordinates' trust both to leaders themselves and to the whole organization.

James C. Collins pointed out in *Good to Great* that leaders who are consistent in words and deeds, unswerving, honest and strong are excellent leaders. Leaders' self-management is closely related to their fame and reputation. It determines largely their influence on employees and the trust their subordinates place in them. What's more, leaders' excellent self-management greatly improves the willingness and motivation of subordinates to do what is assigned to them. Therefore, self-management is known as one of the two cores of followership.

Whenever we talk about professional qualities of an individual, IQ and EQ are always mentioned. Similarly, if leaders expect to develop excellent self-management, they should pay attention to five self-management indicators which are named as a whole as 5Q.

The 5Q of self-management is composed of Discipline Quotient (DQ), Emotional Quotient (EQ), Adversity Quotient (AQ), Moral Quotient (MQ) and Image Quotient (IQ).

- DQ refers to the degree of leaders' self-discipline and self-restraint. It evaluates whether leaders can practice what they preach and whether leaders' behaviors are consistent with the values, regulations and policies of their teams.
- EQ refers to the degree of leaders' effective emotional control in problem solving and relationship building. It also refers to leaders' abilities to stimulate and motivate team members to enhance their enthusiasm and passion in work. What's more, leaders with high EQ have deep insight into the emotional and mental changes of others.
- AQ refers to leaders' abilities, determination and persistence when in difficult situations. Leaders should also encourage, motivate and inspire their team members who are facing adversities.

- MQ refers to the influence of leaders' moralities, personalities and characters on their team members. Leaders need to shape and refine their own unique shining points of morality.
- IQ refers to the degree of leaders' maintenance and refinement on their public appearance and their mental profiles in the minds of their subordinates.

Leaders' behaviors reflected by these 5Qs demonstrate their self-discipline in managing themselves, which is shown in Table 2.1.

There are some excellent leaders who have demonstrated excellent performance in terms of the five indicators of self-management. But actually, lots of leaders need to make further improvements if they are evaluated by the 5Q model. Some even have serious defects or problems in one or some of the 5Qs.

As far as DQ is concerned, Kobe Bryant is a must-be-mentioned example. He used to get up and start his training at four o'clock in the morning when Los Angeles was still in darkness. "Ten years later, the darkness of the streets in LA has not changed, but I have become a muscular, energetic and strong leader of my basketball team," said Kobe.

Indeed, it was not only his talent but also his superb DQ that made Kobe a superstar in NBA history. Leaders with high DQ practice what they preach and are highly self-disciplined. Moreover, they are anxious to be excellent models and examples to be followed by team members. On the contrary, leaders with low DQ always hope to restrict others with higher standards while treating themselves with lower ones.

There is an EQ paradox in leadership and management: the more you are in a frenzy of rage, the less scared your subordinates are of you. On the contrary, the more modest and dispassionate you are, the more fearful your subordinates will be. This paradox illustrates how important leaders' EQ is to the management of their teams. Leaders with high EQ are always energetic, enthusiastic, optimistic and active in front of their subordinates, never showing passiveness or frustration to their subordinates.

AQ is also very critical to leaders. The greater the difficulties and adversities, the more anxious followers are to see what their leaders will say and do. Leaders who are full of high spirits under favorable circumstances but dejected in adversities will be regarded by their subordinates as double-faced persons unworthy of trust. Excellent leaders will consider adversities as precious opportunities to show their persistence and braveness to

TABLE 2.1

5Q Model of Leaders' Self-Management

5Q Model	Leader's Corresponding Behaviors
Discipline Quotient (DQ)	• **Practice What They Preach:** Leaders should maintain high levels of consistency between their words and deeds and refrain from lying or cheating. • **Comply with Policies and Regulations:** Leaders shall set good examples in complying with the regulations, policies and disciplines of their teams and organizations. • **Exhibit Team Values:** Leaders shall exhibit the values of their teams through their own words, behavior and practices.
Emotional Quotient (EQ)	• **Control Emotions:** Leaders need to demonstrate their self-restraint and grace through effective emotional control so as to win respect from their subordinates and others. Many leaders lose recognition from others when they lose control of their emotions. • **Be Enthusiastic and Passionate:** Leaders should positively influence others' emotions and enhance their enthusiasm through showing to others their own passions and proactiveness. • **Care about Others:** Leaders with high EQ are sensitive to the emotional changes in subordinates and offer timely interventions or assistance, making subordinates feel their care, concern and love.
Adversity Quotient (AQ)	• **Be Persistent in Adversities:** When faced with adversities, leaders need to show their character of persistence and braveness. • **Motivate Subordinates in Difficulties:** Leaders shall be good at encouraging and inspiring subordinates in difficulties and stimulating the potential of their teams to overcome difficulties.
Moral Quotient (MQ)	• **Develop Shining Points in Moral Character:** Leaders need to develop their own moral traits and refine their unique shining points in morality and personality. • **Influence Others by Demonstrating Moral Merits:** Leaders shall demonstrate the shining points of their own moral characters on various occasions through words and behavior in order to optimize the characters of subordinates.
Image Quotient (IQ)	• **Shape Public Appearance and Manners:** Leaders shall attach great importance to their dressing, etiquette and manners on various public occasions. Many business leaders have their own image consultants who help position and shape public images for them. • **Maintain and Polish Leadership Profile:** Leaders also need to build good images and impressions in the minds of their team members and keep maintaining and polishing their leadership profiles.

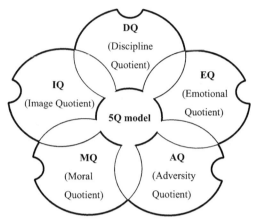

FIGURE 2.2
5Q model of self-management.

subordinates. Their extraordinary achievements or breakthroughs in difficulties will greatly inspire and encourage people around them.

As the old saying goes: you can deceive people for a while but never for a lifetime. In the short run, leaders can win trust and recognition from subordinates by employing strategies or using skills. But in the long run, leaders' moral traits and personal characters will be clearly known to their subordinates sooner or later. As a result, only leaders with high MQ can turn subordinates into long-term followers.

Nowadays there are increasing requirements on image-building for middle-level and senior leaders. Image refers not only to leaders' external appearance but also to the psychological profiles leaders build in the minds of others. Many well-known leaders design and promote their personal images with the help of professional image consultants. Every leader should have his or her own PB (personal brand) which defines what kind of people he or she is in the mind of subordinates. Leaders need to keep maintaining, upgrading and perfecting their PB (Figure 2.2).

SEVEN LAWS OF LEADERS' UPWARD MANAGEMENT

Another core component of followership is upward management, which aims to improve leaders' interpersonal harmonies with and win more support from their superiors. However, many outstanding leaders who are skilled in team management have poor performance in upward management.

Peng Lei, one of the founders of Alibaba Group, is widely known as "the woman behind Jack Ma." As an irreplaceable member of Jack Ma's core team, Peng Lei won consistent trust from her boss. She used to say: "Whatever Jack Ma's decision is, my only job is to make his decision become the most correct one." Her successful career results not only from her outstanding professional abilities but also from her excellent upward management.

How to judge whether a leader is good or bad at upward management? What problems should leaders pay attention to and what rules should they follow in upward management? There are seven laws of upward management which can offer references or new thoughts to leaders.

Upward Management Law I: Understand and Cater to the Behavioral Types of Superiors

Leaders should understand that superiors have different behavioral types. Take decision-making for example, some are arbitrary and dictatorial while others are irresolute and hesitant. Superiors also differ from each other in terms of perspective on interests. Some have long-term visions and development strategies while others only care about immediate interests. Different superiors have different working styles: some prefer to achieve objectives as soon as possible while others insist progress should be made step-by-step.

Clear and correct understanding of the behavioral types of superiors can help leaders better adapt themselves to the preferences of superiors, so that leaders' words and behaviors will be considered more acceptable and trustworthy by their superiors.

Upward Management Law II: Diagnose the Emotional Cycles of Superiors

Most superiors have emotional cycles and the emotional state of superiors will have a great influence on their preferences, judgments and the decisions. Leaders should be sensitive to and make accurate judgments on the emotional changes of their superiors. Based on clear recognition of superiors' emotional cycles, leaders can choose the right timing and most correct contents when communicating with their superiors.

Upward Management Law III: Eliminate the Blind Zones of Superiors' Supervision

As a leader, you should not avoid the supervision of your superiors. On the contrary, you should report to and communicate with your superiors actively, enabling them to clearly know all that you are doing. Most smart leaders are able to make their superiors enjoy such feelings that everything is in control. Leaders should try all means to eliminate the blind zones of superiors' supervision so as to win more appreciation and trust from them. Leaders' communications and interactions with their superiors should be enhanced both formally and informally.

Upward Management Law IV: Provide Timely Support to Superiors

Leaders need to pay close attention to the situation of their superiors and provide timely support to them when superiors face difficulties and challenges. Leaders should not look on indifferently and coldly when superiors run into difficulties. On the contrary, leaders should consider difficult situations of their superiors as precious opportunities of trust-building with them and provide all available support to help superiors who are in adversities. Mutual trust will be improved dramatically when leaders provide timely help to their superiors.

Upward Management Law V: Help Superiors Manage Their Time

Leaders need to understand that the time of their superiors is very precious. Occupying superiors' time frequently with unimportant or trivial things will lead to their boredom and dislike. As a leader, you must learn to manage the time of your superiors and try to minimize interruptions and overly disturbing them. While there is a need to communicate with your superiors, you should check their calendars and make appointments with them. While reporting to superiors, you should summarize key points of your reports and present them quickly.

Upward Management Law VI: Present Problems as well as Solutions

When it is urgent for you as a leader to report to your superiors about emergencies or crises, you should propose solutions and feasible plans at the same time. You should let them know what you have done as well as what you will do to solve the problems. What's more, you should also tell your superiors that you are willing to bear the responsibilities and undertake the consequences for them. In their minds, you are like a firewall in front of them when the fire is spreading.

Upward Management Law VII: Promise What You Are Able to Do

As a leader, you shall not make excessive promises just for the sake of catering to your superiors. Smart leaders always promise no more than what they are able to do because they know that any breach of promise will greatly reduce superiors' trust in them. If you as a leader find it difficult to reject superiors' requirements and demands, you should still try to lower their expectations and warn them of possible risks so that they can prepare alternative plans in advance. The seven laws of upward management can help leaders improve their relationships with superiors, win increasing trust from superiors and maintain smooth communication with superiors (Figure 2.3).

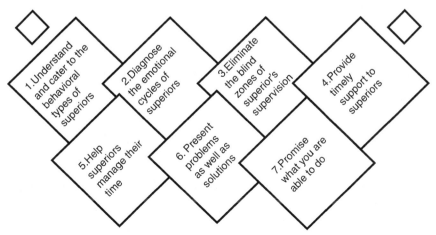

FIGURE 2.3
Seven laws of upward management.

There are some subordinates in the leader's team who can be defined as special superiors due to their non-positional influences sourced from their seniority, personality, professional expertise or mastery of resources. Therefore, these seven laws can also be applied to improve the interpersonal relationships and mutual trusts between leaders and their special superiors. Leaders can switch their leadership modes to upward management when the leadership modes of downward management make these special superiors resistant and even rebellious. Mark Zuckerberg, CEO of Facebook, also followed most of the seven upward management laws while handling his cooperative relationship with Sandberg, COO of Facebook.

Sheryl Sandberg, a superwoman of the Silicon Valley, acted in a quite mighty way since she joined Facebook. She wouldn't even save the face and dignity of Zuckerberg, the CEO. She even went as far as requiring Zuckerberg to report to her on a weekly basis about his working progress. Zuckerberg applied many of the seven upward management laws while communicating with her in order to show his respect to Sandberg and win more support from her. The application of the seven upward management laws to special superiors can be manifested in detail as follows (Table 2.2):

- Leaders should not communicate with special superiors in a mighty and arrogant way. Instead, they should understand and cater to the behavioral types of special superiors, pay close attention to the emotional cycles of special superiors and keep them informed of progress to eliminate their blind zones, which obviously reflects the first, second and third laws of upward management.
- Leaders should offer timely support and resources to these special superiors so as to assist them in getting through crises and enable them to raise their heads proudly in front of others. This is the application of the fourth law of upward management to special superiors.
- Instead of occupying the time of special superiors randomly or assigning insignificant tasks to them, leaders should match them with key tasks or critical assignments which can give full play to their specialties and advantages. This can be regarded as a creative application of the fifth law of upward management.
- Leaders should not be too soft-spoken or submissive while seeking help from special superiors whenever running into problems. If so, leaders will be regarded by special superiors as incapable and may be looked down upon. Instead, leaders should share their experiences,

TABLE 2.2

Self-evaluation of Leaders' Upward Management Ability (Full Score:10)

Do you know clearly whether the decision-making style of your direct superior is democratic-oriented or autocratic-oriented? ( )

Do you know clearly whether your direct superior cares more about short-term interests or more about long-term missions of your team? ( )

Can you know clearly whether your direct superior attaches more importance to his or her own interests or pays more attention to the interests of the whole organization? ( )

Do you know clearly how your direct superior balances between more achievements and less risks in the pursuit of results? ()

Will you always pay close attention to your superiors' emotional changes when you are communicating with them? ( )

Will you adjust and modify the contents or strategies of communications with your superiors according to their emotional states? ( )

Are you able to communicate with or report to your superiors at the right time based on your observation of their emotional changes? ( )

Are you used to regularly and actively reporting to your superiors about your progress so as to make them clearer about your real situation? ( )

Will you become very sensitive and mindful when the attentions paid to you by your superiors are reduced and the frequency of communication between you and superiors is lowered? ( )

Will you prepare and present your work reports carefully so as to make your superiors better know how you are doing recently? ( )

Will you regard it as an opportunity to improve trust with your superiors when you find that they are in difficulty? ( )

Will you communicate with your superiors proactively and show them your willingness to help when you find that they are in adversity? ( )

Are you willing to assist your superiors in coping with challenges and solving problems at the expense of your own interests? ( )

Will you try not to mention your help and support to your superiors in front of others so as to save their faces? ( )

Will you make appointments with your superiors in advance if you need to communicate with and report to them? ( )

Do you agree with the viewpoint that a good subordinate shall try to occupy as little time of his or her superiors as possible if not necessary? ( )

Will you always summarize in advance the key points of your reports so as to present in a time-saving way to your superiors? ( )

When you find that your superiors are kept busy, will you try to share their workloads so as to improve their work efficiency and time management? ( )

When there is a need to report to superiors about crises or emergencies, will you propose solutions and feasible plans at the same time? ()

When reporting to superiors about crises or emergencies, will you also let them know what you have done and what progress has been made? ()

While reporting to superiors about crises or emergencies, will you let them know that you are willing to bear the responsibilities and undertake the consequences for them?

(continued)

TABLE 2.2 (Cont.)

Self-evaluation of Leaders' Upward Management Ability (Full Score:10)

Are you such a person who won't make excessive promises just for the sake of catering to superiors? ( )

Do you think you are such a subordinate who will undoubtedly honor the promises once they are made in the minds of your superiors? ( )

When you find it difficult to refuse your superiors' requests which are hard to be fulfilled, will you try to lower the expectations of your superiors so that they can prepare alternative plans in advance? ( )

---

suggestions and solutions in advance while seeking support from special superiors, making them recognize leaders' professional expertise and working experiences.

- Leaders shall also learn to manage and lower the expectations of special superiors. Expectations of special superiors will be pushed up much higher if leaders are too indulgent and overly satisfying their needs. In other words, leaders shall also abide by the seventh law of upward management while managing special superiors.

Part II

Face-to-Face Leadership

3

Four Driving Wheels of Face-to-Face Leadership

Half a year ago James successfully recruited a management trainee for his marketing department through strict processes of interview and abundant reference checks. This girl named Jenny was open-minded, proactive and aggressive. James found that she was just the kind of high-potential talent he wanted to hire.

After Jenny completed her three-month induction training, James went out of his way to appoint her as the sales assistant of Tom, his regional sales manager. What James wanted to achieve was to cultivate and discipline Jenny at the grassroots level. As James had to study abroad in a three-month leadership training camp, he hadn't inquired with Tom about Jenny's progress because of his strong confidence in her.

James had a face-to-face talk with Tom about the situation and Jenny's progress right after he came back from the training. It was not his expectation that Tom was quite dissatisfied with Jenny for her poor working attitude and inadequate abilities. Tom insisted that Jenny was just like eye candy unworthy of further cultivation and development. James was a bit confused. He couldn't believe that Jenny's performance, which was so excellent in his eyes, would differ so greatly from what he had expected. He firmly believed in his own judgment with regards to Jenny, but he also didn't doubt what Tom had told him. So, what were the main causes of the gap between Jenny's actual working performance and James' original expectation?

James' confusion was closely related to the performance gap of Jenny. Performance gap refers to the obvious gap between subordinates' actual performance and the expectation set by their leaders. In other words, subordinates' performance fails to meet the expected standards set by their leaders.

Performance gaps of subordinates are what face-to-face leaders must pay attention to and deal with. The effectiveness of face-to-face leadership must be measured by whether performance gaps of subordinates have been successfully narrowed or eliminated.

Leaders should be clear about how performance gaps of subordinates are generated and what the main causes behind them are. It was just with such ideas in mind that James invited Jenny for a heart-to-heart talk in person, with an attempt to find the true causes behind her performance gap.

What made James surprised again was the dissatisfaction of Jenny toward Tom who was her direct superior as well. Tom was an absolutely unqualified leader in her eyes. Jenny said, Tom was totally unclear about the specific requirements and operating standards when he assigned working tasks to me. He just kept telling me to understand and think on my own. But not until I did something wrong would he fly into a rage and say that I had no idea of his expectations and requirements. I promise there would be much fewer mistakes or errors if he could make it clearer and more specified while assigning jobs to me.

James agreed with Jenny on the fact that Tom was indeed a person without a logical mind. "The tasks assigned by Tom to me sometimes made me frustrated because many of them were quite insignificant and valueless. He never made clear explanations regarding the jobs to be done, nor was he able to encourage me when I was down," Jenny complained. "Did he offer any help or coaching to you when you were in trouble?" asked James.

> I do hope he can offer me some guidance and help at critical moments. After all, I am a green hand who lacks practical experience in many areas. But he kept insisting that young people should learn from failures and solving problems on their own. In fact, it was hard for me to learn any useful experience from what I've done wrong without timely feedback and instruction from others.

Jenny continued. "He should have offered timely feedback to me and helped me make improvements during the process of execution," Jenny said sadly. "But he did nothing other than blaming, criticizing and even penalizing me when there was something wrong." James was lost in thought again after his talk with Jenny. As Jenny's face-to-face leader, it was Tom's unshrinkable responsibility to evaluate as well as eliminate Jenny's performance gap.

It was obvious in this case that Tom not only failed to eliminate Jenny's performance gap but also worsened it. Tom did not even realize that his own face-to-face leadership was problematic at all since he had never analyzed the main causes of Jenny's performance gap.

Although there may be various causes to Jenny's performance gap, the root ones of them can be generalized into four "don't knows." The four "don't knows" as the root causes of performance gaps should be deeply understood by leaders so as to precisely position and employ their face-to-face leadership.

THE FOUR "DON'T KNOW" ROOT CAUSES OF PERFORMANCE GAP

Face-to-face leadership should be positioned toward the elimination of performance gaps of subordinates, so accurate analysis of the four "don't knows" is the premise and basis of effective face-to-face leadership. Among Jenny's comments on Tom, we can find out the existence of the four "don't know" root causes of Jenny's performance gap, which is described and shown in Table 3.1.

These "Four Don't Know" enable leaders to have clearer understanding of the possible root causes behind subordinates' performance gaps which are just the target of face-to-face leadership. Once face-to-face leaders find that the performance of subordinates is lower than expected, they should learn to diagnose the root causes according to the analysis model of "Four Don't Know" (see Figure 3.1). The performance gap of any subordinate is undoubtedly linked to certain problems arising from one or several of the Four Don't Know. There may be problems resulting from only one of the Four Don't Know for some subordinates, while there may be problems related to many of the Four Don't Know for others.

FOUR DRIVING WHEELS OF FACE-TO-FACE LEADERSHIP

Leaders need to take actions and employ four important tools of face-to-face leadership to eliminate the performance gaps of subordinates caused

TABLE 3.1

Four "Don't Know" Analyses of Jenny's Performance Gap

Jenny's Comments on Tom	Corresponding "Don't Know"
Tom was totally unclear about the specific requirements and operating standards when he assigned working tasks to me. He just kept telling me to understand and think on my own. But not until I did something wrong would he fly into a rage and say that I had no idea of his expectations and requirements. I promise there would be much fewer mistakes or errors if he could make it clearer and more specified while assigning jobs to me.	The first root cause of Jenny's performance gap is don't know what to do. In other words, the work and tasks assigned by Tom are not specific, explicit and clear enough for Jenny to understand, leading to her performance gap which resulted from incomprehension of job requirements or confusion about behavioral directions.
The tasks assigned by Tom to me sometimes made me frustrated because many of them were quite insignificant and valueless. He never made clear explanations regarding the jobs to be done, nor was he able to encourage me when I was down.	The second root cause of Jenny's performance gap is don't know why to do it, which means she did not understand and recognize the meaningfulness and significance of her assignments. In this sense, her performance gap is also caused by insufficient willingness and motivation to carry out what was assigned to her by Tom.
I do hope he can offer me some guidance and help at critical moments. After all, I am a green hand who lacks practical experience in many areas. But he kept insisting that young people should learn from failures and solving problems on their own. In fact, it was hard for me to learn any useful experience from what I've done wrong without timely feedback and instruction from others.	The third root cause of Jenny's performance gap is don't know how to do it. Even if Jenny was talented and had participated in induction training, she still lacked enough on-the-job experience which should be coached and trained by Tom as her direct leader. Hence another cause of Jenny's performance gap was the lack of enough working skills and on-the-job experiences which are needed for the successful accomplishment of assignments.
He should have offered timely feedback to me and helped me make improvements during the process of execution. But he did nothing other than blaming, criticizing, and even penalizing me when there was something wrong.	The fourth root cause of Jenny's performance gap is don't know whether I'm doing well or not. Tom failed to follow up the proceedings following Jenny's execution and provide timely feedback as well as corrections to Jenny's inappropriate behaviors and less-than-expected performances.

TABLE 3.1 (Cont.)

Four "Don't Know" Analyses of Jenny's Performance Gap

Jenny's Comments on Tom	Corresponding "Don't Know"
	In one word, Jenny's performance gap was caused by the lack of timely feedback, follow-up and correction from Tom.

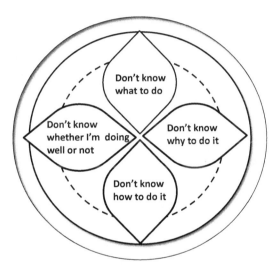

FIGURE 3.1

Four "Don't Know" analysis of subordinates' performance gaps.

by the Four Don't Know. These four tools are also called the four driving wheels of face-to-face leadership, which are boundary-defined delegation, inner-driven motivation, dual-track mentoring and preventative intervention.

- **Boundary-defined delegation:** Mastery of boundary-defined delegation can help leaders ensure subordinates' clear understanding and accurate execution of assignments and restrict the behaviors of subordinates within the boundaries set by leaders. Obviously, boundary-defined delegation is aimed at the elimination of performance gaps resulting from don't know what to do.
- **Inner-driven motivation:** Good command of inner-driven motivation can help leaders implant passions and motivation into

subordinates from the inside out, ensuring that their subordinates have a strong sense of mission and high willingness to execute and accomplish what is assigned to them. Inner-driven motivation is a solution to the elimination of performance gaps resulting from don't know why to do it.

- **Dual-track mentoring:** Mastery of dual-track mentoring can help leaders better prepare and conduct on-the-job coaching needed by their subordinates so as to improve their independence and competence in the process of mission completion. Dual-track mentoring is targeted at performance gaps caused by don't know how to do it.
- **Preventative intervention:** A good grasp of preventative intervention can improve leaders' foresight into and keenness to deal with behavioral deviation in subordinates.

Leaders intervene in subordinates' mission implementation and correct their wrongdoings. Preventative intervention is obviously targeted at performance gaps caused by don't know whether I'm doing well or not.

While using the four driving wheels of face-to-face leadership in practice, leaders need to follow two key principles which are accurate use and combined use (see Figure 3.2). Leaders need to enhance accuracy while using the four wheels of face-to-face leadership. In other words, they should accurately choose and employ one or several of the four driving wheels based on their precise diagnoses of the "don't know" root causes of subordinates' performance gaps.

Subordinates may differ from each other in terms of their "don't know" root causes of performance gaps. Hence leaders should drive different wheels toward subordinates with different don't knows so as to enhance the accuracy of leadership. Accurate use of four driving wheels is people-oriented, while combined use of face-to-face leadership is task-oriented. Four wheels should be used as a whole by leaders to promote the efficiency and effectiveness of execution for significant and urgent missions or projects. For example, if there is a short-term project to be carried out by all the subordinates, leaders should employ boundary-defined delegation first to clearly clarify and publicize the job specifications, performance objectives and working standards to all the subordinates. In the meantime, leaders also need to infuse willingness, motivation, enthusiasm and morale into their subordinates by driving the wheel of inner-driven motivation.

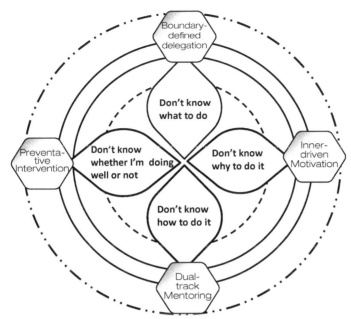

FIGURE 3.2
Four driving wheels of face-to-face leadership.

Leaders should employ dual-track mentoring if they find deficiencies in subordinates' working and mental abilities. What's more, leaders should also pay close attention to the deviation of subordinates' behaviors and take corrective action to narrow the performance gaps of subordinates (preventive intervention).

4

Face-to-Face Leadership: Boundary-Defined Delegation

FORM CLOSED LOOPS OF EXECUTION THROUGH EFFECTIVE DELEGATION

Face-to-face leadership focuses the development of individual subordinates and the improvement of their performance. But unfortunately, many examples consistently show that the inadequate abilities and unsatisfying performances of subordinates result from their leaders' unsuccessful delegation.

Many leadership and management experts may regard delegation as a way for leaders to improve their own work efficiency and time management. While in essence, delegation is a leadership behavior to promote subordinates' execution and performance through transmitting and communicating job specifications and task requirements clearly downward.

Effective delegation is the premise and basis of subordinate's clear understanding of what to do, so it is the primary ability which should be developed by face-to-face leaders. Both insufficient delegation and uncontrolled delegation will cause the behaviors and performances of subordinates to deviate from the right track.

The most important responsibility of a face-to-face leader is to assign periodical missions and tasks downward to lower-level employees and ensure that all their subordinates have accurate understanding of what to do.

If the word delegation is analyzed literally in Chinese, we could break the word down into two characters which include Shou (delegate) and Quan (assignment). Quan (assignment) refers to the goals, missions, plans and tasks to be accomplished by subordinates, while Shou (delegate) means that leaders clearly transmit, publicize and communicate the specification, expectations and standards of assignments downward to subordinates so as to ensure their clear understanding and correct execution.

Delegation defined in this book differs from expressions such as distribution, apportion or allocation. Leaders should not only make sure that subordinates receive the assigned tasks but also make sure that expected accomplishments can be returned. In other words, the objective of delegation is to help subordinates form closed loops at the very beginning period of execution.

The term closed loop has been mentioned frequently in recent years. Closed loop in traditional leadership and management theories normally refers to leaders' behaviors when following up, checking, giving feedback, correction and even firefighting so as to keep subordinates' performances on the expected track during the process of execution.

PDCA cycle, which has been widely advocated and highly recommended, is just an example of traditional closed loop. Leaders assign tasks and plans (P) for their subordinates to do (D). Then in the process of execution, leaders need to check (C) whether subordinates are performing well and provide timely coaching and instructions to correct their action (A).

But unfortunately, this type of closed loop like PDCA will encounter many challenges in real practice. Problems cropping up in the process of a subordinate's execution have already worsened and deteriorated when leaders find them out. Even if leaders take corrective action right after, the optimal timing has already been missed and the cost of problem solving then will be very high. Many leaders are kept playing the role of fire captain while dealing with troubles made by their subordinates.

Leaders should learn to form a closed loop of execution at the period of delegation which is the origin of the whole execution process. To successfully form a closed loop of execution at the period of delegation, leaders are required to set boundaries for subordinates' behaviors while assigning missions or tasks to them.

BOUNDARY-DEFINED DELEGATION

While leaders assign missions or tasks to subordinates, they must define and clarify clear boundaries that subordinates should abide by during

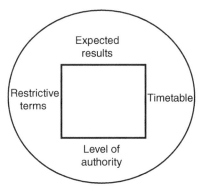

FIGURE 4.1
Four boundaries of delegation.

execution. The performances and actions of subordinates should be strictly restricted within the boundaries set by leaders. If there are no clear boundaries of execution, the behaviors of subordinates will be out of control as they are likely to perform randomly according to their own understanding and willingness.

In China, most leaders adhere to a principle called gentle outwardly but stern inwardly. Being stern inwardly refers to the strict requirements and rules set by leaders which must be respected and obeyed by subordinates. In other words, leaders must clearly define the boundaries of subordinates' behaviors in the process of delegation while being gentle outwardly which means that subordinates can act flexibly and decide on their own for situations outside the boundaries.

There are four key components of the boundaries of execution which leaders should make clear to subordinates, which are expected results, restrictive terms, level of authority and timetable (Figure 4.1).

Expected Results

Leaders must clarify clearly the expected results of the tasks to be accomplished by their subordinates. Expected results can either be qualitative or quantitative but it is better for leaders to make it quantitative. What subordinates should know clearly includes not only what is going to be done but also what results are expected to be achieved.

Restrictive Terms

Leaders set clearly the restrictions or forbidden areas that subordinates cannot overstep while fulfilling their responsibilities. There is no need for leaders to list too many restrictive terms. The fewer restrictive terms there are, the more impressive and unforgettable they will be. Leaders must tell subordinates what they are not allowed to do under any conditions. Restrictive terms define No (what can't be done) instead of Yes (what can be done).

Level of Authority

Leaders should let subordinates know the degree of their autonomy and the level of their authority while they are carrying out the assigned tasks. There are in total five levels of authorities with different levels suitable for different subordinates. The lower the ability level of subordinates, the less the authority granted by leaders will be. Level 1 means the lowest level of authority while Level 5 is the highest level.

Level 1: Subordinates are not allowed to take any actions without approval from their leaders.

Level 2: Subordinates are allowed to propose what to do but can't take any actions before obtaining approval from leaders.

Level 3: Subordinates must report to leaders their action plans and can act whether or not their plans are approved.

Level 4: Subordinates can take action without the approval from leaders, but they need to report to leaders right after their completion of actions.

Level 5: Subordinates can take actions without the approval from leaders, nor do they need to report to their leaders after the completion of actions.

Time Table

Leaders must make it clear to subordinates the due time in the process of their implementation. They must clarify at least two deadlines with one related to when to finish and the other related to when to report results. If tasks assigned to subordinates are complicated and will last for a long period of time, leaders can set several deadlines to check the proceedings of subordinates within the entire implementation cycle.

In fact, many leaders failed to make clear the four boundaries which include expected results, restrictive terms, level of authority and time table to their subordinates in the process of delegation, although the four boundaries seem very simple and easy to use.

There seem to be no problems or mistakes in the following two examples of delegation dialog. But if these two examples are examined by the four boundaries of delegation, it won't be difficult for us to find that there is actually not any boundary in the two delegation dialogs. The lack of boundaries will inevitably lead to high possibilities of mistakes in subordinates' implementation process (Table 4.1).

Leaders can refer to and use Table 4.2 so as to develop good habits of setting boundaries in the process of delegation. In the first column of the table are the tasks and responsibilities leaders need to assign to their subordinates. The second column is to be filled in with the description of forms of delegation adopted by leaders. Forms of delegation may include meeting, face-to-face dialog, telephone call, email, written notice, mobile chat and so on. The third column of the table contains the four boundaries that should be made clear to subordinates, which are expected results, restrictive terms, level of authority and time table (Table 4.3).

Experienced leaders will further improve their instructions and guidance to subordinates on the basis of the four boundaries of delegation by sharing information, resources, challenges and support with their subordinates.

Information

If subordinates need more necessary information due to their unfamiliarity with the assignments, leaders should inform subordinates about related channels or sources of obtaining the information they need.

Resources

Leaders should make known to subordinates what resources are available for them to use for the better accomplishment of tasks. Resources may include tools, equipment, budget, personnel, technologies or policies, and so on.

TABLE 4.1

Two Delegation Dialog to Analyze the Lack of Boundaries

Two Delegation Dialog	Analysis of Lack of Boundaries
Example 1 Mary (Supervisor) said to Rose (Subordinate): "Rose, please go and attend a routine meeting to be held tomorrow. Do your best as you are representing our department." Rose: "Ok, I will."	In this delegation dialog, Mary as the supervisor failed to clarify and make clear all of the four boundaries: • Mary failed to make clear what Rose should bring back to her after attending the meeting. • Mary failed to clarify what Rose was not allowed to do during the meeting. • Mary failed to make clear the level of authority given to Rose when she had to make decisions or take actions during the meeting. • Mary failed to make clear the due time of arriving at the venue and the deadline of reporting results to her after the meeting.
Example 2 Jackson (Supervisor) told Lawrence (subordinate): "Jerry has been inactive at work recently and he has not submitted his work report as required. You should have a talk with him as soon as possible." Lawrence: "No problem."	In this delegation dialog, Jackson also failed to make clear all of the four boundaries: • Jackson failed to specify what results Lawrence should achieve and bring back after talking with Jerry. • Jackson failed to make clear what Lawrence should absolutely refrain from doing while communicating with Jerry. • Jackson failed to specify the level of authority Lawrence was granted when he had to take some actions during his communication with Jerry. • Jackson failed to make clear the due time of Lawrence's completion of talk with Jerry and the deadline of his report to Jackson.

Challenges

Leaders need to remind subordinates of the difficulties, challenges, accidents and setbacks they may encounter in the near future, so that subordinates can make mental preparations as well as alternative plans in advance.

TABLE 4.2

Boundary-defined Delegation

Responsibility Description	Form of Delegation	Four Boundaries of Delegation				
		Expected Results				
		Restrictive Terms				
		Level of Authority				
		Level1	Level2	Level3	Level4	Level5
		Time Table				
		When to finish		When to report results		

TABLE 4.3

Complete Work Table of Boundary-defined Delegation

Task Description						
Name of subordinate						
Form of Delegation	**Four Boundaries**	**Information**	**Resources**	**Challenges**	**Supports**	
	Expected Results:					
	Restrictive Terms:					
	Level of Authority:					
	Time Table:					

Support

Support mentioned here refer to the encouragement from leaders to their subordinates, aimed at making subordinates know their leaders' confidences in their abilities to accomplish tasks and attain objectives. Leaders shall show tolerance toward their subordinates by allowing for mistakes and express their willingness to share the responsibilities with their subordinates.

GUARD AGAINST ANTI-DELEGATION FROM SUBORDINATES

One phenomenon that leaders need to pay attention to and guard against in particular in delegation is anti-delegation, which means that subordinates shuffle their responsibilities and challenges at work the other way around to their supervisors. Thus leaders have to spend time doing what should be done by their subordinates. In fact, the root cause of anti-delegation is the unclear definition of responsibility.

Responsibility is just like a monkey which should be kept on the shoulders of its owners (subordinates), instead of being secretly transferred onto the shoulders of leaders.

Generally speaking, two types of leaders are the likeliest victims of anti-delegation. The first type of leader refers to those who take excessive pride in their own professional abilities. These leaders tend to undertake responsibilities of subordinates in order to prove their prominence and demonstrate their excellence.

Another type of leader refers to those who care too much about their interpersonal relationships with subordinates and are reluctant to say no to requests from subordinates. They tend to help subordinates who are in trouble due to their sympathies toward those subordinates.

While leaders are handling anti-delegation from their subordinates, the following strategies can be referred to and applied in practice:

- **Strategy 1:** Leaders should define clear boundaries of responsibilities and tell subordinates that they should bear their own responsibilities. Leaders only share experiences with them and offer guidance to them if requested.
- **Strategy 2:** Leaders should try their best to boost the self-confidence and self-esteem of subordinates, making them believe in their own capabilities when solving problems.
- **Strategy 3:** Leaders can partition tasks into several subtasks and leave most of the subtasks to their subordinates. Leaders choose to undertake one or a few of those subtasks so they will not have too much of their time occupied.
- **Strategy 4:** Leaders can force subordinates to give up their attempts at anti-delegation by requesting them to satisfy some conditions in exchange.

TABLE 4.4

Five Kinds of Implicit Anti-delegation

Approval-type Anti-delegation	Some subordinates will always ask for approval from their leaders when they are to take certain actions or make some decisions. Such kinds of anti-delegation will result in frequent interruptions in leaders' schedules and severe fragmentation of leaders' time.
Advice-type Anti-delegation	Some subordinates often turn to leaders for advice when they are faced with challenges. Leaders have to spend time finding out solutions for their subordinates if they fail to refuse such kinds of anti-delegation.
Decision-type Anti-delegation	Some subordinates are used to submitting several action plans to their leaders and asking their leaders to choose the right one for them. Such kinds of anti-delegation will help subordinates evade responsibilities of decision-making as well as consequences resulting from wrong decisions.
Problem-type Anti-delegation	Some subordinates never report their mistakes or problems to leaders until there are severe crises or emergencies. Such kinds of anti-delegation will involve leaders fully in the handling of emergencies and the fighting of fires.
Avoidance-type Anti-delegation	Some subordinates will deliberately fabricate time conflict so as to shuffle off responsibilities and shift their tasks onto the shoulders of leaders.

In recent years, there are some implicit behaviors of anti-delegation calling for great attention from leaders. These behaviors do not look like anti-delegation but they do result in the transfer of responsibilities from subordinates to leaders.

There are five kinds of implicit anti-delegation which include approval-type anti-delegation, support-type anti-delegation, decision-type anti-delegation, problem-type anti-delegation and avoidance-type anti-delegation. Leaders should be able to recognize these implicit anti-delegations and deal with them. (See Table 4.4 for the Five Kinds of Implicit Anti-Delegation.)

5

Face-to-Face Leadership — Inner-Driven Motivation

INNER-DRIVEN MOTIVATION VERSUS MATERIAL INCENTIVE

Aiweek, a mid-sized computer company, entered a new stage of development fueled by cut-throat competition. With increasing saturation of market and intensity of competition, Aiweek's business growth ground to a halt. Jeffrey, marketing director of Aiweek, was advised that the enthusiasm of sales teams could be greatly improved and salespeople must be motivated to approach and develop more clients. He decided to adopt and implement MBO (managing by objectives) as a solution to the improvement of salespeople's performance.

Jeffrey set the goal of sales growth at 200% for the new financial year and distributed the sales growth goal to every sales team and then to every salesperson. In the new incentive policy, the bonus of each salesperson would be doubled if the sales team successfully reached the stipulated growth target. But for those sales teams that failed to attain objectives, salespeople could only get 25% of the bonus and their salaries would be cut by 50%.

From Jeffrey's perspective, this new incentive policy could greatly motivate talented salespeople to accomplish the sales growth target in order to get the doubled bonuses. Whereas for unqualified employees who failed to achieve the objectives, the company could also lower the costs wasted on them.

At that time, Aiweek fell far behind its main competitors in various areas such as brand awareness, product competitiveness, technical innovation and after-sale services. None of the company's sales staff had confidence in accomplishing the sales growth target and most of them even had the feeling of being fooled. A year later, none of the sales team was rewarded with the doubled bonus and many excellent salespeople left and joined Aiweek's rivals.

Jeffrey's adoption of MBO was aimed at motivating salespeople and promoting their enthusiasm in new client development. But unfortunately, this new incentive policy not only failed to take effect but also demoralized all the salespeople. Jeffrey took it for granted that salespeople would be greatly stimulated and motivated in the face of attractive monetary rewards. But a phenomenon which leaders should pay special attention to is that there won't necessarily be positive correlations between material incentives and the inner drive of employees.

Great leaders are those who can motivate and inspire subordinates by arousing their inner drive whenever they are in serious shortage of monetary rewards and material incentives. Leaders have to learn what on earth the components of subordinates' inner drive are if they desire to upgrade from material incentive to inner-driven motivation.

FOUR TYPES OF INNER DRIVE

Inner-driven motivation can fully unleash the potential of subordinates by creating four types of inner drive (Figure 5.1). Inner drive of meaningfulness, inner drive of ownership, inner drive of return and inner drive of self-confidence constitute the complete toolbox of motivation which can be used by leaders.

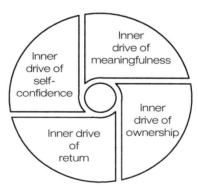

FIGURE 5.1
Four types of inner drive.

Inner Drive of Meaningfulness

When subordinates believe what they are doing is meaningful and significant, their inner drive derived from a sense of responsibility and mission will be greatly boosted. We can find in the following story that people with a different sense of meaningfulness toward the same task differ from each other in terms of inner drive.

There were three workers who were building a wall. Someone passed by and asked worker A, "What are you doing?" Worker A answered, "I'm building a wall." The passerby turned to ask worker B, "What are you doing?" "I'm building a house," worker B answered. When the passerby continued to ask worker C the same question, worker C replied happily, "I'm so excited that we are building a church which will be a landmark building here. People living around will have a comfortable gathering place. I'll try my best to make it perfect."

Obviously, these three workers had different inner drives of meaningfulness although they were engaged in the same work. As a result, their morale and enthusiasm in building the wall differed greatly. Likewise, employees performing the same task in the same team may have different levels of inner drive because their sense of mission and sense of value are quite different. Hence, leaders should improve subordinates' realization and understanding of the significance and meaningfulness of the missions assigned to them. For those jobs or assignments which are considered by subordinates to be insignificant or meaningless, leaders should be able to amplify their sense of self-worth and sense of duty.

Inner Drive of Ownership

Subordinates with a sense of participation, decision-making, autonomy and freedom are more likely to devote themselves to the accomplishment of missions assigned by leaders. Akito Morita, chairman of the board of Sony, was used to dining and chatting with his employees in the staff canteen in order to build good rapport with them. One day, Akito Morita found a young employee who ate silently and seemed quite depressed. Akito Morita walked to the staff member and started to talk to him. After several cups of drinks, this employee finally told him the reason for his unhappiness.

> I graduated from the University of Tokyo. Before I joined Sony, I was in frantic admiration of Sony. At that time, I believed it was the best choice in

my life to be a member of Sony. However, it is not until now that I find that I am not working for Sony but for my section supervisor. Frankly speaking, my section supervisor is not a trustworthy leader because he shows no respect to his subordinates at all. We are not allowed to express our own opinions for any of his arrangements and absolute obedience is emphasized by him time and again. What's more, he forbids us from proposing any suggestions and offers us no right to act on our own. We are just like robots working under his supervision.

What Akito Morita learned from his talk with this young employee was that subordinates will be demotivated dramatically once they lose a sense of autonomy in their working environments. In other words, leaders should motivate subordinates through increasing their inner drive of ownership.

Inner Drive of Return

When subordinates believe that their accomplishment of the missions assigned by leaders can bring them satisfying returns and rewards, their inner drive will be greatly stimulated. On the contrary, if subordinates lose hope of winning expected rewards through accomplishing certain tasks, their self-motivation and morale will be dramatically reduced.

There are three main factors which determine subordinates' sense of return. The first factor is the amount as well as content of rewards that employees can obtain. The second factor is the probability of obtaining expected rewards and the third one is how long will it take for employees to get the expected rewards.

An automotive manufacturing enterprise headquartered in Europe enacted its new incentive policy of product innovation to promote the morale of technical staff in developing new products. In the previous policy any staff whose innovative methods were adopted would be rewarded a bonus which would be paid within three months. The bonus of the new incentive policy tripled that of the previous one but would be paid a year later after the innovation was put into application.

Surprisingly, the morale of technical staff reduced greatly after this new policy was promulgated. The technical team's inner drive of return dropped although the amount of bonus had tripled. The main reason for such negative impact is that the payment cycle of bonuses was greatly lengthened and the possibility of winning the reward was dramatically lessened. Return here includes not only salary, bonus and other material rewards but also honor, promotion, career development and other interests in a broad sense.

Inner Drive of Self-confidence

When subordinates have full self-confidence in achieving objectives and accomplishing tasks, they will be high in spirits and their morale will rise. On the contrary, if subordinates feel it quite difficult and challenging to complete the assigned tasks no matter how hard they try, their morale and self-motivation will decrease greatly.

A well-known expert in education visited a primary school. Before he left, he wrote down the names of several students on a list and told the headmaster and teachers of this school that these students would make extraordinary achievements in the future. Decades later, his prediction came true. These students whose names were on the list had indeed become famous scientists, entrepreneurs and educationalists. By this time, people had started to wonder how this expert had managed such accurate predictions. The expert answered with a smile: I just wrote down several names randomly.

TABLE 5.1

Evaluation Sheet of the Four Types of Inner Drive

1. Totally disagree 2. Strongly disagree 3. Disagree 4. Neutral 5. Agree 6. Strongly agree 7. 100% agree

    a. I have full confidence in my ability at work.

    b. What I am doing currently is very important and meaningful to the overall performance of my organization.

    c. I have enough autonomy in determining the ways to do my own work.

    d. My excellent working performance can change the fate of my family and myself.

    e. The work I'm engaged in can give me a sense of mission and excitement.

    f. My performance at work will be appreciated by my superiors and I will have the opportunity of getting promoted.

    g. I have got enough respect as well as right to make suggestions in my organization.

    h. My superiors always encourage me to raise constructive advice and suggestions.

    i. I believe that my organization has given me enough support and resources for the accomplishment of my tasks.

    j. The work I am doing can positively influence and impact a lot of people.

    k. My ability and personal growth will be greatly enhanced through accomplishing tasks.

    l. I feel that the difficulty of doing my job well is within my expectation.

Why could the students randomly selected by the expert really make great achievements? Self-confidence is the answer. Confidence was transferred from the expert to the headmaster and teachers of the school and then to these selected students. Due to their strong self-confidence in attaining outstanding achievements, students listed by the expert were highly motivated and inner-driven. These four types of inner drive can accurately analyze why the leadership behaviors of some leaders boost the morale of employees and why others cannot.

In the case of Aiweek, the new incentive policy impacted the morale of salespeople negatively because it lowered their inner drive of return and inner drive of self-confidence. Such an incentive measure was not only useless but also destructive.

For leaders who want to know the self-evaluation of subordinates in terms of the four types of inner drive, Table 5.1 can be applied to investigate and understand the levels of inner drive in their subordinates. Leaders can evaluate and improve their own performances on employee motivation accordingly.

6

Face-to-Face Leadership— Dual-Track Mentoring

TWO MAJOR TRACKS OF SUBORDINATE'S ABILITY

Adam was recently appointed as the sales manager of a new business unit in his company. He found that in his team there was a senior sales representative named Benson whose sales performances were even worse than those of some new staff. Benson had failed to accomplish sales targets for two consecutive months. What's more, his visit records and sales funnel analysis showed that there were no more new clients or new sales leads created by him. During a routine co-visit to clients with Benson, Adam was surprised by the excellent communication and selling skills of Benson. He demonstrated outstanding capabilities in the fields of trust building, product introduction, troubleshooting or deal closing. Adam held a face-to-face talk with Benson right after the coordinated visit. At the beginning of their communication, Adam kept inquiring about the detailed information of each client based on Benson's visit records.

Benson did reply with abundant information for some key accounts he was familiar with. But later on, when asking about the progress of some other clients, Adam found that Benson was totally unfamiliar with them although the names of these clients were listed on his visit records. Adam then asked Benson a critical question: "Have you failed to visit clients recently?" Benson remained silent for a while and replied, "Yes." Adam then asked him for the reason.

At that moment, Benson knew that he had to tell Adam the truth. He said that he had been a sales representative of another business unit for four years. Due to his continuous efforts at developing new accounts and building trust with all the existing clients, Benson's sales performance was the best among all the members of his team. But he was later replaced by the son of a vice president and forced to leave his team and join Adam's business unit.

He felt the fruits of his labor had been stolen by others. Therefore, he became very passive and inactive in developing new clients as he believed that his achievements would still be robbed by others in the future. In Adam's original plan before the co-visit, he had thought about sharing with Benson his own selling skills and strategies on new client development, but now he found that the problem didn't lie in Benson's working ability, but in his mental ability.

Take railway tracks as an example: there should always be two tracks supporting the steady driving of any train. Trains will be derailed if there are problems with either one of the two tracks. It is also true for the subordinate's abilities which are made up of two indispensable tracks. One is working ability and the other is mental ability.

What leaders can learn from Adam and Benson's case is that they should first analyze whether the poor performances of subordinates resulted from their working capabilities or their mental abilities before they get down to mentoring their subordinates. Subordinates with inadequate working abilities need effective coaching while those poor in their mental abilities need timely counseling. Coaching and counseling are considered as two major tracks of a leader's mentoring of subordinates. In this case, Adam finally found that what Benson needed most was not coaching for his working ability, but counseling for his mental ability. So what are the specific differences between coaching and counseling? In Table 6.1, the basic definitions and main differences between these two are listed in detail.

FORMS AND RULES OF PERFECT COACHING

Excellent coaches in the NBA always call timeout at critical moments in order to coach their players by sharing with them valuable tactics and skills. NBA coaches have different types of timeout for different purposes. Leaders can do similarly by choosing different forms of coaching according to different kinds of situations.

TABLE 6.1

Coaching Versus Counseling

Coaching	Counseling
Coaching refers to leader's behaviors of experience sharing and skill development for the sake of improving the working abilities and performance of subordinates.	Counseling refers to leader's behaviors of psychological intervention and mood regulation in order to solve the mental problems of subordinates and improve their mental abilities.
Coaching focuses on solving problems resulting from subordinate's lack of knowledge, skills and working abilities.	Counseling focuses on solving problems caused by subordinate's unhealthy mentalities and negative moods.
Coaching is generally prepared and planned by leaders in advance.	Counseling tends to be triggered unexpectedly. It often takes place without enough preparation in advance due to leaders' lack of necessary information.
In the process of coaching, leaders share with subordinates their experiences, solutions, guidance and even demonstrations to help them better solve problems or deal with challenges.	In the process of counseling, leaders release subordinates' pressures, pacify their emotions and optimize their mentalities through active listening and positive feedback.
To improve the effectiveness of coaching, leaders can invite a third party to join in the process of coaching.	In counseling, in order to ensure confidentiality and the sense of security, the third party who leaders invite in should already have enough mutual trust with the target subordinate.
In coaching, leaders can achieve results by following the steps preset in coaching plans.	In counseling, there may not be preset steps or plans and leaders' efforts in counseling may not produce results.

Four Types of Situational Coaching

Leaders can categorize the situations of coaching into four based on two dimensions. The first dimension is whether the problems that leaders need to solve by coaching are personalized problems of individuals or common problems of most team members. The second dimension is whether there are mature experiences and existing solutions available for leaders to share with their subordinates.

Based on these two dimensions, the situations of coaching can be divided into four, including common problems with mature experiences available, common problems without mature experiences available, individualized problems with mature experiences available and individualized problems without mature experiences available. Leaders can adopt four types of coaching in accordance with these four situations, which are assembled training, brainstorming salon, individual tutorship and collaborative work (Figure 6.1).

1. In situations featured by common problems with mature experiences available, the problems are common ones existing in most subordinates and leaders have mature experiences and solutions to share with them. Leaders can convene assembled training attended by most team members and ask subordinates to learn, master and apply in practice their prepared counterplans or solutions. Such type of coaching does not call for team members to raise their own opinions and suggestions. Attendees of assembled training are asked to learn carefully the provided experiences and action plans and put them into practice as quickly as possible.

2. Leaders with neither existing experiences nor mature solutions can organize brainstorming salons for common problems of team members. All members of a leader's team are brought together to

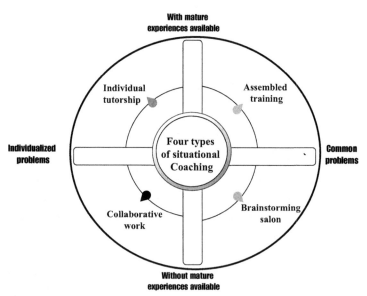

FIGURE 6.1
Four types of situational coaching.

brainstorm. Subordinates are encouraged to discuss openly and freely any possible solutions and countermeasures. The key to the success of salon-type of coaching lies in leaders' capabilities of guiding team members toward open discussions and creative thinking.

3. For individualized problems for which leaders have mature experiences and solutions, individual tutorship can be adopted by leaders as a way of coaching. Leaders share their own experiences and suggestions with individual subordinates and set action plans for them.

4. As for individualized problems for which leaders have no mature experiences and solutions, collaborative work is the best coaching method to adopt. Leaders must enter into the real working scenarios of subordinates, offering suggestions, solutions, demonstrations or support to them on the spot.

It is noteworthy that there is a one-to-one match between four types of coaching and four coaching situations. In other words, mismatch between the types of coaching and the situations of coaching may result in dissatisfying results. For example, if leaders with no existing solutions or mature experiences convene assembled training and force subordinates to learn some outdated, inappropriate or even impractical countermeasures and skills, their subordinates will feel it a waste of their time. Besides, once subordinates find that even their leaders are not able to offer useful solutions or help, their morale will drop rapidly.

Five Key Rules of Perfect Coaching

No matter which one of the four types of coaching is adopted, there are five key rules that leaders should follow in order to improve the effectiveness of coaching (Table 6.2). Leaders should not cover too many subjects in each coaching session but focus on one or two main problems of subordinates at most. Focusing on one or two subjects is the first rule of effective coaching. Leaders must try to highly refine the contents of coaching and make them as simple as possible. The more simplified the contents of coaching are, the more effective a leader's coaching will be and the more willing their subordinates are to put them into practice. This is the second key rule called simplifying the contents of coaching.

TABLE 6.2

Five Key Rules of Perfect Coaching

Five Key Rules	Special Requirements
Focus on One or Two Subjects	• All coaching provided by leaders shall not involve too many subjects but focus on one or two problems to be addressed by subordinates. • The subjects in each coaching session should be closely related to the biggest problems or weakest points of the subordinates so that performance improvements can be achieved rapidly.
Simplify the Contents of Coaching	• The content of leaders' coaching must be refined, summarized and simplified as much as possible at the end of each coaching. • Leaders can achieve the simplification of coaching content by using graphics, tables, gestures, slogans, etc.
Orient at Behavioral Change	• The objectives of leaders' coaching need to be upgraded from having subordinates know what it is to enabling them to know how to do it. • The fruits of leaders' coaching should be transformed into specific action plans and behavioral steps. • Leaders should also provide subordinates with lists on which actions to be taken after the coaching are specified.
Test the Usefulness of Coaching In Practice	• Leaders must require subordinates to put into practice what they have learned as quickly as possible. • Leaders must try to test and examine whether the skills and tactics learned from the coaching can truly help subordinates address their problems. • Leaders need to ask subordinates about their feedback after they have put the coached skills into practice.
Follow Up with Reinforcement Coaching	• Leaders should prepare and conduct follow-up coaching for the same subject if they feel it necessary. • Leaders need to strengthen, improve and perfect the learning effects of their subordinates with follow-up coaching. • Leaders can correct, optimize and refine the contents of the previous coaching through follow-up coaching.

The objective of leaders' coaching should be upgraded from knowledge and skill improvement to behavioral change and correction, which is the third rule of effective coaching known as orienting at behavioral change. Leaders must require their subordinates to put what they learn into practice so as to examine whether learned experiences and skills can truly solve their problems. Leaders need to ask for feedback from their subordinates during their application of coaching achievements. Testing the usefulness of coaching in practice is the fourth rule.

It is necessary for leaders to prepare and carry out follow-up coaching based on the feedback from the first-time coaching. Follow-up coaching can help subordinates consolidate, improve and perfect what they have learned from the previous coaching. This is the final key rule of effective coaching called following up with reinforcement coaching.

MODES AND PRINCIPLES OF EFFECTIVE COUNSELING

In the minds of many leaders, the capabilities of subordinates refer only to their working abilities and professional skills. But many cases indicate that working abilities and professional skills will be devalued and even become destructive without their synergy with mental abilities. Leaders should play the role of psychologists in their teams and provide timely counseling to their subordinates. The main purpose of counseling is to help subordinates release negative emotions, lessen unnecessary pressures and rebuild healthy moods.

Four Modes of Situational Counseling

There are different situations in which leaders should employ different modes of counseling. Situations of counseling can also be categorized into four based on two dimensions. One dimension is the extent to which the target subordinate is willing to share with leaders his or her real mindset and inner emotions. Another dimension is the extent to which leaders are capable of conducting counseling on their own. Based on these two dimensions, there are in total four situations of counseling which are defined as follows (Table 6.3):

Situation 1: Target subordinates are willing to speak their mind and leaders are capable of conducting counseling on their own.

Situation 2: Target subordinates are willing to speak their mind but leaders are incapable of conducting counseling on their own.

Situation 3: Target subordinates are unwilling to speak their mind but leaders are capable of conducting counseling on their own.

Situation 4: Target subordinates are unwilling to speak their mind and leaders are incapable of conducting counseling on their own.

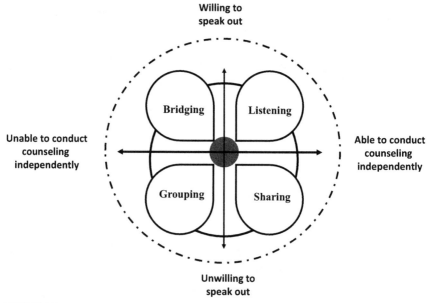

FIGURE 6.2
Four modes of situational counseling.

Leaders should adopt appropriate counseling modes to match these four situations (Figure 6.2).

- The best mode of counseling in situation 1 is listening. Leaders play the role of listeners and encourage target subordinates to share with them their experiences, thoughts, feelings and complaints. Leaders' active listening can help subordinates release their negative emotions and rebuild self-confidence.
- The best mode of counseling in situation 2 is bridging. Leaders invite in a third party to facilitate the counseling as a bridge. Target subordinates may be willing to speak their mind because of the interpersonal trust between the third party and them. The third party can be family members, friends, colleagues and schoolmates of the subordinates or professional psychologists.
- The best mode of counseling in situation 3 is sharing. Leaders take the initiative in sharing with target subordinates their experiences, feelings and understanding when they were in similar situations. Subordinates' emotional resonances may be triggered by such

TABLE 6.3

Four Situations and Corresponding Modes of Counseling

Situation	Definition	Corresponding Counseling Mode
Situation 1	Target subordinates are willing to speak their mind and leaders are capable of conducting counseling on their own.	**Listening:** Leaders play the roles of listeners and encourage target subordinates to share with them their experiences, thoughts, feelings and complaints.
Situation 2	Target subordinates are willing to speak their mind but leaders are incapable of conducting counseling on their own.	**Bridging:** Leaders invite in a third party to facilitate the counseling as a bridge.
Situation 3	Target subordinates are unwilling to speak their mind but leaders are capable of conducting counseling on their own.	**Sharing:** Leaders take the initiative in sharing with target subordinates their experiences, feelings and understanding when they were in similar situations.
Situation 4	Target subordinates are unwilling to speak their mind and leaders are incapable of conducting counseling on their own	**Grouping:** Leaders participate in some group activities together with the target subordinate so as to lessen their psychological pressures and release their negative emotions.

common experiences and they will be more likely to speak out their own mind.

- The best mode of counseling in situation 4 is grouping. Leaders participate in some group activities together with target subordinates. Group activities can include sports activities, social activities, conferences, gathering, and so on. Participation in these activities can greatly lessen psychological pressure and release negative emotions in target subordinates.

Four Principles of Effective Counseling

Leaders should act as psychological doctors for their teams and provide timely counseling to subordinates who have problems in their mental abilities. But counseling, different from coaching, will not necessarily be productive and may sometimes even trigger conflicts. Excellent psychological

TABLE 6.4

Four Principles of Effective Counseling

Four Principles	Specific Descriptions
Focus on Emotions	• Leaders should pay attention to emotions rather than actual problems. • Leaders should show their sympathies and convey their concerns to subordinates in a heartfelt way. • Leaders should focus on releasing the negative emotions of subordinates, instead of finding ways to solve their problems and deal with their challenges.
Express in a Positive Way	• The same viewpoints of leaders can be expressed either positively or negatively. But in psychological counseling, all leaders' viewpoints should be expressed in a positive way. • Leaders expressed their recognition and understanding to the feelings of the subordinates but not to their viewpoints and doings. • The objective of positive expression in counseling is to trigger subordinates' self-motivation and rebuild their self-confidence.
Excavate Subordinate's Resources	• Leaders should understand that each target subordinate has the willingness to make changes and improvements. Hence leaders need to encourage target subordinates to excavate their available resources and solve problems on their own. • Leaders should not impose solutions or action plans on the target subordinate but try to guide him or her toward suitable solutions.
Respect Boundaries of Counseling	• Leaders must be clear about the boundaries of counseling that define what can be done by them and what should be done by the target subordinate. • Leaders should pay attention to the degree of intervention in the emotional and psychological problems of subordinates. Sometimes excessive interventions during counseling may lead to endless troubles.

doctors always follow some critical principles so as to make their counseling more effective and fruitful.

The effectiveness of counseling can be examined by four major principles which leaders should follow. These four principles focus on emotions, expressing in a positive way, excavating subordinate's resources and respecting boundaries of counseling, which are shown in Table 6.4.

7

Face-to-Face Leadership—Preventive Intervention

BEHAVIORAL INTERVENTION VERSUS PERFORMANCE ASSESSMENT

Face-to-face leaders must learn to act as navigators or monitors of their teams in order to evaluate and improve the behaviors as well as performances of subordinates. Under many circumstances, subordinates are unable and unwilling to check as well as eliminate the gaps between their own performances and leaders' expectations. Leaders must ensure that their subordinates are advancing smoothly on the preset performance tracks. Once any possibility of derailment is discovered, leaders must intervene in time and take corrective action so as to prevent problems from getting worse.

More importantly, such interventions and corrections must be conducted in a preventive way instead of being done in a fire-fighting way. In other words, leaders should intervene and take corrective action before the consequences of subordinates' derailed behavior become worse.

In ancient China, there was a well-known doctor called Bian Que. The emperor of his kingdom used to ask Bian Que, "Why is your family able to cultivate such a peerless and highly skilled doctor like you?" Bian Que said,

> Your Majesty, there are things you don't know. In fact, I have two brothers in my family and all three of us have become doctors. As far as medical skills are concerned, my eldest brother is the most excellent and I'm the worst among the three.

The emperor answered in confusion: "It's impossible. Your reputation is known to everyone in the world. To be frank, I have never heard of your two older brothers." Bian Que continued to explain,

> My eldest brother would prescribe medicine and root out the diseases before their outbreaks. Most of his patients were even unaware of their sicknesses, so it is difficult for him to obtain recognitions from others. Therefore, he is not famous but only greatly admired within my family. My second elder brother usually starts treatment at the beginning of diseases when the symptoms are not obvious and the patients do not feel much pain. People around him take it for granted that he is only good at curing minor illnesses. I don't cure diseases until they have become quite severe. By that time, the patients become very painful and their families worry too much. I treat in extreme ways such as puncturing the meridians, releasing blood with needles or applying poisons to the wound to fight against poisons. In this way, patients who get their symptoms relieved or be cured will regard me as an excellent doctor.

To monitor and control the behaviors and performances of subordinates, lots of managers depend largely on performance evaluations and assessments. But for those outstanding leaders, they prefer to intervene in employees' process of execution and take corrective actions earlier.

Ordinary managers with insufficient insight or foresight in future changes and possible consequences will often rely heavily on performance evaluations and assessments, the opposite from excellent leaders who can predict severe consequences of employees' behaviors which seem non-destructive at present. Behavioral intervention and performance appraisal, as two ways of monitoring subordinates' progress, differ from each other in many areas (Table 7.1).

Murphy's Law suggests that anything that can go wrong will eventually go wrong. Therefore, leaders must never believe in luck when it comes to potential crises and possible problems. They should intervene in advance before situations become worse.

Leaders are always busy and they are not able to intervene in every-thing, no matter how important. Their attentions should be paid to and focused on subordinates' behaviors which seem not serious at present but are likely to deteriorate. These behaviors conform to Murphy's Law so they are named as Murphy's Behaviors.

TABLE 7.1

Behavioral Intervention versus Performance Appraisal

Behavioral Intervention	Performance Appraisal
On a random basis.	On a periodical basis.
Take actions before the results come out.	Take actions after results come out.
Rely on instincts and prejudgments of leaders.	Rely on data, facts and details.
Small prices and strong timeliness.	Big prices and longer time lag.
Leaders prefer behavioral interventions.	Managers prefer performance appraisals.

FIVE MURPHY'S BEHAVIORS IN URGENT NEED OF INTERVENTION

Murphy's behaviors must be behaviors that seem not serious in the beginning but will lead to severe consequences without intervention. There are five types of Murphy's behaviors which leaders should pay special attention to (Figure 7.1). They are Murphy's behaviors of setting negative examples, Murphy's behaviors of breaking the work chain, Murphy's behaviors of violating iron laws, Murphy's behaviors of accelerating performance degradation and Murphy's behaviors of sowing the seeds of calamity (Table 7.2).

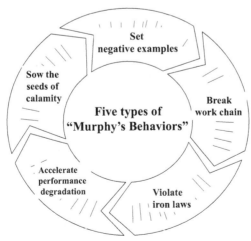

FIGURE 7.1
Five types of Murphy's behaviors.

If the deviant behavior of subordinates could cause other team members to follow suit and result in severe consequences for the group, leaders should intervene in and correct such Murphy's behaviors of setting negative examples in time.

If subordinates' duties are parts of a complete execution chain, then any minor behavioral error of theirs will lead to the breakdown of whole execution chain. In other words, behavioral errors of individuals will have negative impacts on performances of others who work together with them. Leaders should pay close attention to such Murphy's Behaviors of breaking work chain.

If some subordinates openly violate and disobey the core disciplines repeatedly stressed by leaders, nonintervention in or non-correction of such behaviors will greatly damage leaders' prestige and authority among team members. Subordinates may no longer earnestly abide

TABLE 7.2

Five Murphy's Behaviors in Urgent Need of Intervention

Five Murphy's Behaviors	Detailed Definition
Murphy's behaviors of setting negative examples	The individual behavior of subordinates produces negative demonstrations and sets destructive examples to those around who may follow suit. Subordinates' individual behaviors may turn into group behaviors rapidly without leader's intervention and correction.
Murphy's behaviors of breaking the work chain	Inappropriate behavior of subordinates can cause destruction and damage in the whole execution chain if there are no timely interventions and rectifications from leaders. The work chain referred to here may be either lateral or vertical.
Murphy's behaviors of violating iron laws	If the behaviors of some subordinates are in flagrant violation of the core disciplines or policies stressed repeatedly by leaders, the personal authority of leaders and the credibility of other disciplines or policies will be greatly damaged if there are no interventions in or corrections to these behaviors.
Murphy's behaviors of accelerating performance degradation	Failure of subordinates to meet certain performance standards or requirements for the first time may form a vicious cycle of performance degradation if leaders ignore them.
Murphy's behaviors of sowing the seeds of calamity	As long as the behavioral mistakes of subordinates are related to morality or law, they should be intervened in and corrected as soon as possible, no matter how slight in severity they are. Ignorance of them is just like sowing the seeds of calamity.

by other requirements and commands from their leaders. Therefore leaders should attach great importance to Murphy's behaviors of violating iron laws.

If some subordinates fail to reach one or certain standards of performance for the first time, their leaders must intervene and meddle in a mighty way. Leaders should urge subordinates to reflect on their failure and take corrective action. Once leaders are unable to intervene in the first-time failure of subordinates to reach certain standards, their subordinates will be likely to enter a vicious cycle of performance degradation naturally. Leaders should learn to identify such Murphy's behaviors of accelerating performance degradation.

Leaders must intervene in and correct the behavioral errors of subordinates which involve issues pertaining to morality or law. Even if those issues are not severe and have not caused serious consequences, leaders should understand that ignorance of them equates to sowing the seeds of trouble. Such issues must result in severe consequences if they happen again. This kind of Murphy's behavior is sowing the seeds of calamity.

SEVEN GOLDEN STEPS OF INTERVENTION INTERVIEW

To intervene in and correct these Murphy's behaviors mentioned above, leaders need to arrange and conduct formal face-to-face interviews with subordinates to discover problems and find solutions. However, intervention interviews happen to reflect the lacking in many leaders. Without appropriate steps and processes, many intervention interviews may lead to contradictions and conflicts.

Some leaders choose to overlook and sidestep the Murphy's behaviors of subordinates just because they lack the relevant intervention interview skills. Leaders need to abide by the hamburger rule or the sandwich rule during intervention interviews. As requested by the hamburger (or sandwich) rule, an intervention interview is divided into three parts, just like hamburgers (sandwiches) with meat (pork, beef, etc.) placed in the middle of bread. Similarly, in a hamburger-style (sandwich-style) intervention interview, leaders should first express recognition, respect and gratefulness to their subordinates (bread) and then point out their mistakes which should be corrected (meat). At the end of the intervention interview, expectations, encouragement and gratefulness (bread) should be expressed again by leaders to their subordinates.

Hamburger-type and sandwich-style intervention interviews address different problems and are used under different circumstances. It is better for leaders to adopt sandwich-style intervention interviews for first-time mistakes or minor errors by using more bread (recognitions, affirmations and gratefulness) and less meats (problem discussions, criticisms and corrections). Leaders should adopt hamburger-style intervention interviews for frequent offenses and serious problems by using more meat (problem discussions, corrections, sand punishments) and less breads (recognitions, affirmations and gratefulness).

Hamburger (sandwich)-style intervention interviews can be divided into seven golden steps (Table 7.3), each of which has its unique objective and effect.

Step 1: Show Recognition

Leaders show recognition and express gratitude to their subordinates for their past performances and contributions so as to relieve their tensions and avoid opposition between both sides.

TABLE 7.3

Seven Golden Steps of Successful Intervention Interviews

Seven Steps	Leader's Behaviors
Show recognition	Step I: Show recognition & respect and express gratitude to subordinates
Present facts	Step II: Prepare and present detailed facts of behavioral errors on the part of subordinates in an open way
Amplify seriousness	Step III: Expound and amplify the consequences and negative influences of the behavioral errors of subordinates
Review previous expectations	Step IV: Look back with subordinates on the previous expectations on them and review the consensus between both sides
Get promises	Step V: Require subordinates to make oral or written promises concerning their improvements of behaviors
Provide support/ Set punitive measures	Step VI: Provide support and resources (sandwich) or set punitive measures (hamburger)
Express gratitude and encouragement	Step VII: Express gratitude to subordinates and give them encouragement

TABLE 7.4

Self-evaluation Questionnaire of Seven-step Intervention Interviews

Choose one of your intervention interviews as an example and evaluate your performance in each step

Steps of Intervention Interviews	Your Self-evaluation
Step I: Show your recognition & respect and express gratitude to subordinates	• While the intervention interview begins, will you show your recognition toward your subordinates for their performance and contributions firstly? () • At the beginning of the intervention interview, are you able to make your subordinate relaxed and relieve their stresses? () • As soon as the intervention interview begins, can your subordinate feel your frankness and sincerity? ()
Step II: Prepare and present detailed facts of behavioral errors on the part of subordinates in an open way	• Can you keep yourself objective and neutral while you are showing the facts of your subordinates' behavioral deviations? () • Are you able to clarify specifically, explicitly and clearly while you are presenting the facts of your subordinates' behavioral deviations? () • Can you control your emotions and speak peacefully while you are pointing out the mistakes or problems of your subordinate? ()
Step III: Expound and amplify the consequences and negative influences of the behavioral errors of subordinates	• Are you good at amplifying the negative consequences of your subordinates' mistakes and problems? () • Are you able to make your subordinate understand that his/her behavioral deviations will be harmful both to the organization as a whole and to himself/herself as an individual? ()
Step IV: Look back with subordinates on the previous expectations on them and review the consensus between both sides	• Will you look back with your subordinate on the previous expectations on him or her? () • Will you express higher expectations and anticipations to your subordinate's future performance? () • Will you compare the recent performances of your subordinate to what was expected from him/her? ()
Step V: Require subordinates to make oral or written promises concerning their improvement of behavior	• Will you discuss with your subordinate ways of behavioral improvement and ask for action plans from him or her? () • Will you require your subordinate to make promises for the agreed improvement plans? ()

(continued)

TABLE 7.4 (Cont.)

Self-evaluation Questionnaire of Seven-step Intervention Interviews

Steps of Intervention Interviews	Your Self-evaluation
	• Will you ask your subordinate to make written promises or publicize his/her promises? ()
	• Will you ask your subordinate to appoint someone who will monitor whether he/she has honored the promises? ()
Step VI: Provide support and resources (sandwich) or set punishments and penalties (hamburger)	• If it is a sandwich-style intervention interview, will you show actively your willingness to offer your subordinate help, support and resources? ()
	• If it is a hamburger-style intervention interview, have you reached consensus with your subordinate on the punitive measures in case he or she fails to honor the promises? ()
Step VII: Express gratitude to subordinates and give them encouragement	• Will you express gratitude to your subordinate at the end of the intervention interview? ()
	• Will you express appreciation to your subordinate for his/her willingness to improve behavior and make promises? ()
	• Will you encourage and motivate your subordinate to implement the improvement plan as promised? ()

Step 2: Present Facts

Leaders should focus on and discuss with subordinates the facts which have been seen, heard, collected or investigated, instead of making subjective as well as negative comments on subordinates. Leaders need to make full preparations and collect objective and persuasive facts for upcoming intervention interviews in advance.

Step 3: Amplify Seriousness

Leaders should amplify the seriousness of subordinates' mistakes and misconduct so as to deepen their realization of the negative consequences of their behavior and the necessity of making improvements.

Step 4: Review Previous Expectations

Leaders review together with their subordinates on the consensus of performance expectations reached by both sides, aiming at obtaining subordinates' acknowledgments that their behaviors have deviated from the right track.

Step 5: Get Promises

Leaders shall require subordinates to make promises on behavior corrections and performance improvements. If necessary, subordinates are asked to publicize their promises so as to test whether they are willing to make improvements or not. Whether leaders can obtain subordinates' promises or not is critical to the success of intervention interviews.

Step 6: Provide Support/Set Punitive Measures

Hamburger-style intervention interviews differ from sandwich-style ones in the sixth step. In hamburger-style interviews, leaders need to reach consensus with subordinates on the punitive measures in case they fail to honor their promises. While in sandwich-style intervention interviews, leaders need to inquire what support and resources their subordinates want from them to ensure they are capable of fulfilling their promises.

Step 7: Express Gratitude and Encouragement

In addition to showing gratitude to subordinates for their willingness to correct mistakes and make promises, leaders should also express their hopes, blessings and encouragement to subordinates (Table 7.4).

Part III

Indirect Leadership

8

Three Major Roles of Indirect Leaders

UPGRADE FROM FACE-TO-FACE LEADERSHIP
TO INDIRECT LEADERSHIP

When the overall number of direct reports managed by leaders exceeds the optimal management span, face-to-face leadership is no longer suitable for large-scale teams. In this case, leaders have to convert their roles from face-to-face leaders to indirect leaders and upgrade their leadership gear from face-to-face leadership to indirect leadership.

The effectiveness of face-to-face leadership depends on whether leaders have sufficient time and energy to conduct detailed, comprehensive and in-depth one-on-one management for each team member. Face-to-face leaders have to spend much time building personal trust with each subordinate and employing the four wheels of face-to-face leadership to develop each member of their core teams.

Leaders of large-scale teams should upgrade their leadership gears. In addition to developing direct reports with face-to-face leadership, leaders should also master the employment of indirect leadership to manage those team members who do not report directly to them.

Many middle-level or grassroots managers find that their original leadership skills no longer take effect once they are promoted to higher positions. They are used to influencing and driving each team member with one-on-one leadership skills even if the teams managed by them are large-size and multilevel.

Take the maintenance of gardens for example. Face-to-face leaders are like gardeners who pay attention to the luxuriant growth of every tree, while indirect leaders are similar to those who focus on the vigorousness of the whole garden. Indirect leaders are devoted to improving the overall performance of their teams rather than the individual performance of subordinates. They will try all means to enhance the centripetal force, executive force and cohesive force of their teams as a whole.

In particular, when leaders are promoted from grassroots supervisors to middle-level managers or even higher positions, it does not mean that face-to-face leadership is completely replaced by indirect leadership. In fact, face-to-face leadership is still needed by leaders to manage direct reports while indirect leadership featured by one-to-many management is targeted at developing indirect reports and the whole teams.

Both face-to-face leadership and indirect leadership are developed and adopted by leaders to promote the performance of their organizations. But they differ from each other in terms of performance development in several areas which are listed in Table 8.1.

TABLE 8.1

Face-to-Face Leadership versus Indirect Leadership

	Face-to-Face Leadership	Indirect Leadership
Object of Leadership	Subordinate as an individual.	Team as a whole.
Condition of Adoption	When the number of team members is within the optimal management span.	When the number of team members exceeds the optimal management span.
Objective of Leadership	Maximize the individual performance of each subordinate.	Maximize the overall performance of the whole team.
Leadership Behaviors	Employ one-on-one leadership behaviors featured by direct interaction with subordinates such as delegation, motivation, coaching, counseling and intervention.	Adopt one-to-many leadership behaviors featured by the enhancement of team's centripetal force, executive force and cohesive force so as to promote the overall performance of leaders' teams.
Perspective of Leaders	Focus on eliminating performance gaps and satisfying development needs of direct reports.	Concentrate on promoting the overall performance and competitiveness of the whole team.
Source of Leadership	Face-to-face interactions and mutual influence between leaders and subordinates.	Visions, values, regulations, mechanisms, behavioral standards, interpersonal trust and emotional bonds shared by each member of the team.
Fruits of Leadership	Capable and loyal direct reports.	High-performance teams.

TABLE 8.2

Two Types of Performance

Micro Performance	Macro Performance
• Leaders are devoted to improving and maximizing the individual performance of each subordinate in their teams. • Actually, the maximization of subordinate's individual performance does not naturally lead to the maximization of overall performance of the whole team.	• Leaders are committed to enhancing the overall performance of their teams instead of improving the individual performance of their subordinates. • More attention are paid to the development of the whole team rather than the growth of individuals.

It is shown obviously in Table 8.1 that face-to-face leadership focuses on the individual growth of each direct report while indirect leadership concentrates on the overall performance of the whole team. Leaders should understand that the upgrade from face-to-face leadership to indirect leadership refers not only to the promotion of managerial position but also to the transformation of performance improvement perspective.

Still, take gardeners who are responsible for the maintenance of large-scale gardens for example. They have to shift their attention from the healthy growth of every tree to the overall vigorousness of the whole garden. There are two types of performance which should be distinguished and recognized by leaders (Table 8.2). Micro performance is aimed at the maximization of individual performance of each subordinate while macro performance is targeted at the maximization of overall performance of the whole team. When the leadership gear is shifted from face-to-face leadership to indirect leadership, leader's perspective on performance improvement should also be upgraded from micro performance to macro performance.

WWH ANALYSIS MODEL OF MACRO PERFORMANCE

The larger the size of a team, the more important it is for leaders to analyze and improve the overall performance of the whole team from the macro perspective. The success of small-team leadership depends mainly on leaders' refined management of individual subordinates, whereas the success of large-team leadership is largely determined by leaders' efforts in the improvement of macro performance. Leaders can analyze and evaluate the overall performance and competitiveness of their teams from three perspectives, which are why, what and how (WWH).

- The first perspective is WHY—Why does our team exist? Does our team have common visions, common values and common commitments which are understood, accepted and shared by all the members?
- The second perspective is WHAT—What do we do together? Is each member of the team clear about his/her key responsibilities, job specifications, working procedures and behavioral standards?
- The third perspective is HOW—How are we related to each other? Do members of the team communicate and interact with each other smoothly? Has interpersonal synergy or mutual trust been built and enhanced inside the team?

These three perspectives can also be named as the WWH analytical model of macro performance (Figure 8.1). Indirect leaders should learn to analyze and evaluate the macro performance of their teams with the help of WWH model.

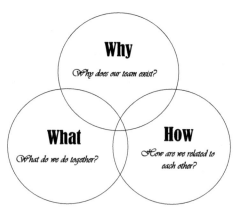

FIGURE 8.1
Three perspectives on macro performance.

TABLE 8.3

Evaluation Form of the Macro Performance of Your Team

1	2	3	4	5
Never	Rarely	Sometimes	Often	Always

Evaluation Form of the Macro Performance of Your Team

Please evaluate the performance of your team based on the following descriptions. According to the rating scale below, please write down the answer on the line ahead of each description (Table 8.3).

1. Why does our team exist?

    _____Team members share a common vision.

    _____Team members have similar understanding in the common vision of our team.

    _____Team members all accept the overall strategies of our team.

    _____ Team members know their own influence on the future of our team.

    _____Team members can clearly describe and deeply understand the values of our team.

    _____Team members live up to the values of our team and insist that others do the same.

    _____The goals of future development are very clear to members of our team.

    _____Team members are committed to the accomplishment of common goals.

2. What do we do together?

    _____There are working procedures understood and followed by team members.

    _____Working procedures are streamlined, specified and standardized.

    _____The roles and responsibilities of team members are clearly defined.

    _____Members abide by the collaborative mechanisms of our team.

    _____Courses of action and behavioral guidelines are available to improve efficiency.

_____Authorities, responsibilities and interests of team members are clearly defined.

_____Resources are allocated efficiently and fairly to support the work of team members.

3. How are we related to each other?

_____There is mutual trust between team members.

_____The working environment is active and friendly within the team.

_____Team members are supportive to each other at work.

_____Team members recognize the contribution of others to the team.

_____Team members listen to others' opinions and freely express their viewpoints.

_____Team members handle conflicts effectively in a win–win way.

_____Team members have common interests, common habits and common hobbies.

THREE KEY ROLES OF INDIRECT LEADERS

A mid-year management salon was convened with the attendance of ten regional sales managers of FP Company at a resort to promote their understanding of leadership. There was a hot debate between the participants on a question raised by Professor Hanks, an expert of management. The question seemed quite simple. What role should you play in your team? "I am a sales champion so I can help my salespeople by solving problems they are faced with in the selling process. Therefore, I believe that my expertise in sales is critical to the success of a sales manager," said Lawrence.

Adam raised his own viewpoint:

> Regional managers are the middle-level executives of our company, so "maintaining stability" is our main responsibility. We shall ensure that everything is in order and on the right track. My efforts in maintaining stability are highly valued by my boss.

"I don't agree with either of you. I believe that the essential role that a regional manager should play is to show team members clear vision, direction and course of action," said Bryant in a different opinion. Bradley insisted that he would spend more time on formulating rules, regulations and working standards for team members to follow. Rule of man should be replaced by rule of law, he added. Bill, Bradley's good friend, held on to his own opinion that regional managers should be like patriarchs who could bind members together and improve interpersonal synergy in their teams.

Professor Hanks expressed his thankfulness to everyone and said:

> Your understanding of the main responsibilities of a regional sales manager exhibits the role you are playing in your team as a leader. Totally, there are five leadership roles which include expert, manager, pioneer, architect and coach. Lawrence attaches great importance to the role of expert while Adam pays much attention to the role of manager. Bryant considers the role of pioneer to be most important and Bradley insists on playing the role of architect. Finally, patriarch in the eyes of Bill equals to the leadership role of coach.

In this case, Professor Hanks summarized five roles leaders usually play in their teams. Different roles exhibit different behaviors and have different contributions to the whole team, which is described in Table 8.4.

There are one-to-one correspondences between three of the five leadership roles and three perspectives of the WWH analytical model of macroperformance. Obviously, the role of pioneer corresponds to the perspective of Why (why does our team exist). The role of architect matches the perspective of What (what do we do together) and the role of coach is closely linked to the perspective of How (how are we related to each other). It is clear that role of pioneer, role of architect and role of coach are just the three key leadership roles which should be strengthened and enhanced by indirect leaders to improve the macro performances of their teams (Figure 8.2).

THREE PERFORMANCE INDICATORS OF INDIRECT LEADERSHIP

Andrew, director of a core business unit affiliated to a listed company, managed a team with over 500 employees. Recently Andrew found that

TABLE 8.4

Behavioral Characteristics of Five Leadership Roles

Leadership Roles	Behavioral Characteristics of Each Role
Manager	• Control the processes and results of work • Plan, organize and monitor to better accomplish tasks • Keep discipline and order • Prefer to maintain the status quo instead of seeking changes
Expert	• Have outstanding professional abilities and logical thinking • Spend lots of time on solving tough problems and handling emergencies • Act as firefighters who help others deal with crises • Prefer to be treated and respected as specialists or professionals
Pioneer	• Have foresight in future changes and development trends • Establish and promote visions, missions, values and strategies of the team • Make the blueprint of team development recognized and shared by all members • Link the current situation of each team member to the future of the whole organization
Architect	• Focus on optimizing organizational structures and working procedures • Formulate disciplines, regulations and rules so as to keep the behaviors of team members on the right track • Establish collaborative mechanisms to improve cross-functional cooperation • Make efforts to upgrade the whole working system
Coach	• Promote interpersonal synergy inside the team • Build mutual trust between team members • Enhance the cohesion of the whole team • Improve member's sense of belonging and loyalty

the performance of the whole team was increasingly deteriorating. What's more, he felt it was quite difficult for him to do well in the management of such a large-scale team.

Andrew tried to find out his own problems and weaknesses in team management and explore effective ways of self-improvement. Then he turned to Bob, a well-known leadership professor, for advice. Bob listened carefully to Andrew's experience and then asked him a question: "What do you think is the greatest difference between the management of a large-scale team and that of a small-sized team?"

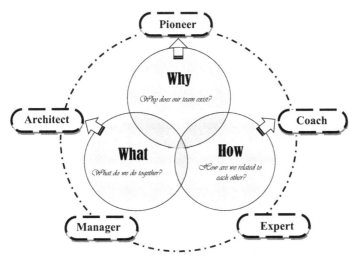

FIGURE 8.2
Three key roles of indirect leaders.

Andrew was confused, "I think there shall be no difference."
Bob said,

> They differ a lot from each other. It is critical for leaders to manage as many details as possible for small-sized teams while it is significant for them to focus on key performance indicators while managing large-scale teams. As far as you as an indirect leader are concerned, I believe it's necessary for you to analyze and examine the main performance indicators of your team as a whole.

Andrew could not wait to ask, "Professor, could you please tell me what on earth are the key performance indicators of large-size teams like mine?" Bob asked, "Have all the employees signed labor contracts with your company?" "Of course!" answered Andrew. Bob continued,

> Then is there a "psychological contract" signed between each member of your team and the organization led by you? Labor contracts are printed on paper, while psychological contract is rooted in the hearts of your employees. "Psychological contract" reflects employees' commitments to and expectations on their organization, which can produce strong centripetal force and self-motivation in the hearts of employees and maintain their sustainable passions at work.

Andrew became silent. Bob added,

> Are the members of your team, especially staff working at key positions, clear about the performance expectations to them from the organization and the standards of execution for their daily work? Will they still perform effectively and correctly if there is no guidance or monitoring from you? You as the leader should learn to improve the execution of employees by setting "performance signposts" guiding them toward the right destination, just like you setup a navigation system onto your car.

"That's just what I'm lacking," Andrew acknowledged. Bob continued,

> I was told that most of the employees you've chosen were quite talented and qualified due to your careful selection and assessment. Do these first-class employees cooperate well with each other? Do they have harmonious relationships with each other? Is there enough mutual trust between them? Are there internal frictions and conflicts in your team? As a leader of such a large-size team, you should try all means to build rapports between team members and minimize disharmony as well as inconsistencies. "Interpersonal synergy" is another performance indicator of large teams which I have frequently stressed.

"Dear professor, psychological contract, performance signpost and interpersonal synergy must be the three main performance indicators of large-size teams. What you just summarized suddenly enlightened me and now I know what I am supposed to do," Andrew said with a smile of confidence on his face.

As an outstanding leadership expert, Bob pointed out that the management of large-sized teams should focus on key performance indicators rather than on details. What's more, he summarized the three key indicators of the macro performance of large-scale teams, which are psychological contract, performance signpost and interpersonal synergy. Coincidentally, the main responsibilities of three key roles of indirect leaders are closely linked to the three performance indicators of indirect leadership. The main responsibility of pioneer is just to establish and strengthen psychological contracts between employees and their organizations so as promote the centripetal force of the whole team.

TABLE 8.5

Three Performance Indicators of Indirect Leadership

Psychological Contract	• Psychological contract reflects the commitment of team members to the goals and missions of their organization, which is a key indicator of the team's centripetal force. • Once employees have signed psychological contracts with their leaders, their mindsets, behaviors, performances and self-expectations will be in high accordance with the future development of the whole team.	Corresponding Leadership Role: **Pioneer** Objective of Team Development: **The centripetal force of the whole team**
Performance Signpost	• Indirect leaders should install on each of their team members a behavioral navigation system to ensure the performance of everyone is on the expected track. Such a navigation system can greatly promote the executive force of the whole team, which is called as performance signpost. • Due to the guidance as well as warning of performance signpost, the behaviors and performances of team members will be kept on the expected track even if there is no face-to-face supervision, coaching, correction or follow-up from leaders.	Corresponding Leadership Role: **Architect** Objective of Team Development: **The executive force of the whole team**
Interpersonal Synergy	• Interpersonal synergy is an indicator measuring the team spirit of and mutual trust between team members. • Indirect leaders should bind together team members with various cultural backgrounds or behavioral styles and improve the overall cohesive force of their teams.	Corresponding Leadership Role: **Coach** Objective of Team Development: **The cohesive force of the whole team**

The key duty of architect is to set performance signposts for all team members in order to enhance the executive force of the whole team. While the role of coach is mainly accountable for promoting the interpersonal synergy between team members for the sake of promoting the cohesive force of the whole team (Table 8.5).

TABLE 8.6

5-Point Rating Scale

1	2	3	4	5
Rarely	Occasionally	Sometimes	Regularly	Frequently

SELF-EVALUATION FORM OF FIVE LEADERSHIP ROLES

Here are seventy questions listed below. Please read each one carefully and select the description which matches your own behaviors. Use the 5-point rating scale and circle the number that accords with your choice (Table 8.6).

Note: The validity of this survey is based on the truthfulness and objectiveness of your answers. All your answers will be strictly kept confidential and won't be shared with others.

HOW DO THE BEHAVIORS IN THE FOLLOWING TABLE MATCH THOSE OF YOURS?

In order to rate the results of this evaluation, please fill in the following table with the number you choose. You will find the corresponding relationship between your choice and the seven main categories below. Add the score of every category and divide the sum with 10, you can get the average score of each category (Tables 8.7 and 8.8).

TABLE 8.7

1	2	3	4	5	1. Spend more time on technical work or business-related work than on managerial work
1	2	3	4	5	2. Good at planning and organizing of the work to be done
1	2	3	4	5	3. Analyze and predict the environmental changes and development trends of your organization
1	2	3	4	5	4. Normalize and standardize working procedures
1	2	3	4	5	5. Eliminate contradictions between team members
1	2	3	4	5	6. Have clear understanding of your influence to others
1	2	3	4	5	7. Act as a collaborator of others in your organization
1	2	3	4	5	8. Exhibit first-class professional skills and problem-solving abilities
1	2	3	4	5	9. Integrate as well as align resources (equipment, personnel or budget) for the successful completion of team's mission
1	2	3	4	5	10. Convey explicitly the vision of your team to your team members
1	2	3	4	5	11. Establish appropriate mechanisms (information-sharing mechanism, rewarding, punitive mechanism, etc.) for the successful implementation of strategies and plans
1	2	3	4	5	12. Encourage others to participate in group activities
1	2	3	4	5	13. Seek as well as accept others' comments on your advantages and weaknesses
1	2	3	4	5	14. Show respect to everyone in your organization
1	2	3	4	5	15. Prefer to do things by yourself
1	2	3	4	5	16. Set short-term objectives and priorities for the effective implementation of plans
1	2	3	4	5	17. Encourage and enlighten others through sharing your vision with them

(continued)

TABLE 8.7 (Cont.)

1	2	3	4	5	18. Change and improve the existing working processes
1	2	3	4	5	19. Motivate team members to cooperate with others
1	2	3	4	5	20. Seize opportunities of improving your own knowledge and skills
1	2	3	4	5	21. Be honest and sincere while communicating with others
1	2	3	4	5	22. Diagnose problems successfully with effective analytical methods
1	2	3	4	5	23. Examine and follow up the performances of others
1	2	3	4	5	24. Transform the vision of your organization into clear business objectives and plans
1	2	3	4	5	25. Explore ways of finding out work contents or working processes which are valueless and time-wasting
1	2	3	4	5	26 Pay attention to the interpersonal harmony between team members
1	2	3	4	5	27. Take actions proactively instead of being guided by others passively
1	2	3	4	5	28. Build harmonious relationships with others
1	2	3	4	5	29. Address problems and deal with challenges for others
1	2	3	4	5	30. Spend lots of time on completing reports and paperwork
1	2	3	4	5	31. Formulate action plans for the realization of business objectives
1	2	3	4	5	32. Seek better ways of working by referring to the experience of other organizations
1	2	3	4	5	33. Improve the willingness of team members to assume the duties of others and solve problems for others
1	2	3	4	5	34. Shoulder full responsibility for not finishing your work on time
1	2	3	4	5	35. Listen to other's opinions carefully and show your respect to their viewpoints

TABLE 8.7 (Cont.)

1	2	3	4	5	36. Try hard to look for and find out the root causes of problems
1	2	3	4	5	37. Correct the mistakes of employees if they violate certain regulations
1	2	3	4	5	38. Challenge conventions and embrace changes
1	2	3	4	5	39. Keep strengthening and improving your own positive attitude
1	2	3	4	5	40. Punish or even fire team members who are harmful to team spirit
1	2	3	4	5	41. Refrain from making excuses or blaming others when you have done something wrong
1	2	3	4	5	42. Treat others in a respectful and sincere way
1	2	3	4	5	43. Search for and evaluate a series of solutions before taking actions
1	2	3	4	5	44. Hold productive and constructive meetings on a regular basis
1	2	3	4	5	45. Communicate with others about the reasons of promoting reforms and changes?
1	2	3	4	5	46. Help establish and transmit the values of your team and your organization
1	2	3	4	5	47. Spend much time on promoting the cohesiveness of your team
1	2	3	4	5	48. Manage your time efficiently and effectively
1	2	3	4	5	49. Motivate and inspire others when they face adversities
1	2	3	4	5	50. Prefer to do things by yourself instead of seeking helps from others
1	2	3	4	5	51. Hold your team members accountable for their own performances and results
1	2	3	4	5	52. Have big pictures of the future changes and development trends of your organization

(*continued*)

TABLE 8.7 (Cont.)

1	2	3	4	5	53. Find out better tools to solve challenging problems
1	2	3	4	5	54. Ally with informal leaders in your organization
1	2	3	4	5	55. Set good examples to others for the promotion of values
1	2	3	4	5	56. Solve conflicts and address problems in an open and flexible way
1	2	3	4	5	57. Make decisions based on sufficient information
1	2	3	4	5	58. Try to maintain everything on the expected track
1	2	3	4	5	59. Encourage adventures and innovations
1	2	3	4	5	60. Challenge policies and practices which are incompatible with the values and business philosophies of your organization
1	2	3	4	5	61. Promote communication and interaction between team members
1	2	3	4	5	62. Honor the promises you have made
1	2	3	4	5	63 Pay close attention to your interpersonal relationship with team members
1	2	3	4	5	64. Skilled at repairing things (equipment, machine, tools, systems, etc.)
1	2	3	4	5	65. Attach great importance to details
1	2	3	4	5	66. Help clear the obstacles of efficient working for others
1	2	3	4	5	67. Appraise the performance of your team and your organization periodically
1	2	3	4	5	68. Improve the teamwork spirit of employees
1	2	3	4	5	69. Control your emotion successfully when you are faced with crises or emergencies
1	2	3	4	5	70. Care about other people's impression of you

TABLE 8.8

	Expert	Manager	Pioneer	Architect	Coach	Self-management	Interpersonal Relationship
	1	2	3	4	5	6	7
	8	9	10	11	12	13	14
	15	16	17	18	19	20	21
	22	23	24	25	26	27	28
	29	30	31	32	33	34	35
	36	37	38	39	40	41	42
	43	44	45	46	47	48	49
	50	51	52	53	54	55	56
	57	58	59	60	61	62	63
	64	65	66	67	68	69	70
Sum							
Averaged Score							

9

Enhancement of the Centripetal Force of a Team

THE 3V TOOLS OF PSYCHOLOGICAL CONTRACT

In teams with strong centripetal force, members must have signed psychological contracts with their organizations in addition to labor contracts. All team members are committed to the accomplishment of missions and goals of their organizations.

Psychological contract is a term opposite to labor contract. Once employees join leaders' teams, they have both expectations on and commitments to the organization. Some of these expectations and commitments can be presented clearly in written forms and specified in labor contracts. The other parts of an employee's expectations and commitments cannot be specified in the form of a labor contract and can only exist in the minds and hearts of employees, which should be embodied in a psychological contract.

Psychological contract is a hot topic in the field of organizational behavior science and HR management. Moreover, it is a key indicator which shows the loyalties of employees and the centripetal force of leader's team. Once employees have signed psychological contracts with their leader, their mindsets, attitudes, behaviors and performances will be oriented in high accordance with the development direction of the whole team.

The effect of psychological contract on the improvement of the centripetal force of a team is self-evident, which can be summarized as follows:

- *Effect of compass*—Psychological contracts are like compasses installed in the minds of employees, showing them the right directions and correct ways.

- **Effect of ruler**—Psychological contracts are like rulers that enable employees to measure the gaps between their own performance and the expectations from their organizations. More importantly, these rulers are not imposed from above but needed by employees themselves.
- **Effect of magnet**—Psychological contracts help leaders attract and unite employees who have common values and mutual interests with their teams. Team members will lag behind or even choose to leave if there are huge gaps between their individual needs and the overall needs of their teams, making it easier for leaders to discover any bad apples and get rid of them quickly.
- **Effect of identity**—Once employees have signed psychological contracts with their teams, they will be more likely to place identities as team members ahead of identities as individuals. They will think of themselves as inseparable parts of teams rather than independent individuals.

Leaders can establish psychological contracts between employees and their teams through the employment of three important tools which include vision anchor, value root and victory chain. As the initial letter of each tool is V, these three tools are also named as the 3V tools of psychological contracts (Table 9.1).

VISION ANCHOR

Jack Welch, Former CEO of General Electric (GE), believed that leaders should develop tempting visions for their teams and try all means to make everybody understand and accept them through continuous promotion and publicity.

An attractive vision can motivate and inspire each member of the team to strive for the realization of it. Visions are like the Big Dipper in the sky, guiding people who walk at night. Visions are like the navigation lights in the sea, telling boats the right directions. Organizations without visions are like trains without locomotives, not knowing where to go.

Effective visions are just like powerful anchors which tightly connect the current situations of employees with the future development of their

TABLE 9.1

The 3V Tools of Psychological Contract

3V Tools	Definition and Description
Vision Anchor	Leaders should set clear visions and make them universally recognized and accepted by all team members. Visions cannot only help employees understand the future directions of action but also promote their sense of mission and responsibility. Excellent visions are like powerful anchors which firmly connect the current behaviors of employees with the future development of their teams.
Value Root	The performance of an employee is just like the vitality of a tree. The quantity and quality of fruits depend largely on the roots of trees. Similarly, the performances of team members are mainly determined by their beliefs and values. Leaders are responsible for shaping the core values of their teams and promoting them continuously so as to influence the thinking and behaviors of employees from the inside out.
Victory Chain	Leaders can use the victory chain to link the growth of employees and the success of their teams together. The successful rotation of the victory chain is driven by mutual commitment between employees and their leaders. Employees shall make commitments to the accomplishment of their performance objectives set by leaders while leaders should also be committed to supporting the personal growth and career development expected by employees.

organizations. Common visions shared by all members are indispensable determinants of successful team development. Great leaders always set and promote attractive visions as a way to stimulate the inner drives of employees.

However, it is a great pity that the visions of many organizations are unable to be accepted and shared by their employees although they can be found on websites, publicity materials or elsewhere. It is no exaggeration to say that only visions of a small portion of organizations can be called vision anchors which are effective in terms of leadership.

Effective vision anchors can greatly drive the improvement of employees' current behaviors toward the direction expected by leaders. In other words, visions which are unable to drive the change of employees' current behaviors can't be regarded as vision anchors. Only the setting, transmission and promotion of vision anchors can be considered leadership behaviors.

Three Major Approaches to Setting Effective Vision Anchor

Is it a one-way vision or a common vision? Is it a virtual vision or a realizable vision? Is it a vague vision or a clear vision? Answers from employees to the above questions can determine whether a vision is a true vision anchor or an invalid vision. The main differences between vision anchors and invalid visions are listed in Table 9.2.

Common vision, realizable vision and clear vision are three main components of effective vision anchors, which leaders should understand deeply while setting and promoting visions. Whether visions can generate the effect of anchor or not is not determined by leaders' own perceptions but by the recognition and acceptances from employees.

Indirect leaders shall not only understand the features as well as effects of vision anchors, but also master the main approaches to setting vision anchors. There are three approaches that leaders can choose from for the successful establishment of vision anchors.

TABLE 9.2

Invalid Vision versus Vision Anchor

Invalid Vision	Vision Anchor
One-way Vision Visions advocated by decision-makers and top managers of the organization are not recognized and accepted by most of the employees.	**Common Vision** Visions of the organization are universally shared by most employees from top to bottom and are recognized by employees as their own.
Virtual Vision Visions of the organization are considered by most employees to be unrealizable, infeasible and unworthy of trust.	**Realizable Vision** Visions of the organization are considered to be achievable, authentic, trustworthy and desirable in the eyes of most employees.
Vague Vision Visions of the organization are unclear, ambiguous, unspecific and unimpressive to most employees. They are rarely mentioned, repeated and publicized by leaders.	**Clear Vision** Visions of the organization are attractive, clear, unforgettable and specified to most employees. They are repeatedly mentioned, reviewed, strengthened and promoted by leaders.

Combining Way of Vision Setting

Leaders unite people together with similar visions to form a team, thus agreements will be quickly and easily reached on the common visions of the team. Such common visions do not have to be extracted, promoted and publicized by leaders deliberately, since the personal visions of each team member are in high accordance with the overall visions of the team. Visions of political parties, associations, social groups, communities and volunteer groups are mostly established through such a combining way.

Extracting Way of Vision Setting

Leaders discuss with members possible visions of the whole team and try to narrow disagreements between different members on a step-by-step basis. Consensus are reached and common visions of the team are confirmed based on the summary and extraction of varieties of alternatives. If members show willing to involve themselves in the process of vision establishment and there isn't great divergence in members' personal visions, leaders of such teams can choose the extracting way of vision setting.

Radiating Way of Vision Setting

Leaders turn their personal visions into the common visions of their teams. They try to seek members' understanding and acceptance of their personal visions. Personal visions of leaders are promoted as their teams' common visions and are recognized and shared by all team members. If most members lack enough cognition of future visions and their willingness to involve in the process of vision establishment is low, leaders of such teams can choose the radiating way of vision setting.

The effectiveness of vision anchor depends not only on whether leaders can choose the appropriate approaches to setting visions but also on whether visions can be promoted and publicized successfully. Leaders need to communicate, transmit and publicize visions of their teams from top to bottom continuously. What's more, leaders should link the personal interests of employees with the visions of their teams and make the realization of visions convincing and credible.

FABTE Mode of the Publicity of Vision Anchor

A cat was very hungry when a salesman came and showed him a pile of money. "Mr. Cat, here is a large amount of money up to a total of USD 10,000." But this cat did not make any response. As the cat became much hungrier, the salesman then said again, "Mr. Cat, this is a pile of cash! It can be used to buy lots of fish! But the cat still did not say anything." The cat got hungrier and hungrier and the salesman continued, "Mr. Cat, look, I have a pile of money here that can allow you to buy a lot of fish. You can use it to buy the freshest fish or any other foods you want to eat." The cat opened his eyes, stood up and looked at the money for a while. However, he finally lay down again.

The cat went extremely starving and the salesman continued his persuasion, "Mr. Cat, look! You can buy enough fish and completely get rid of your hunger and starvation." The eyes of the cat were opened wide. He circled around the money for a few times but still hesitated.

The salesman went on, "Mr. Cat, your girlfriend has just bought herself fresh fish with the money I gave to her. She must be enjoying fresh and delicious fish now. You can go to ask her if you don't trust me." Mr. Cat jumped to the pile of money immediately. It is obvious in this story that the salesman links the value of money with the benefits to the cat step by step. In the beginning he emphasized that the amount of money was USD 10,000, which was the feature of money. Then the salesman said that the money could be used to buy fish, which was the advantage of money. Afterward, the salesman told Mr. Cat that he could buy the freshest fish or other foods with the money, which was the benefit money brought to the cat. Next, the salesman added that Mr. Cat was able to get rid of starvation with the help of money, which was the trouble that money can eliminate for Mr. Cat. Finally, the salesman told Mr. Cat that his girlfriend was enjoying the fish bought with the money, which was the evidence to prove the authenticity of what the salesman said.

The FABTE (Feature, Advantage, Benefit, Trouble and Evidence) mode of vision publicity can be applied by leaders to promote and publicize visions inside their organizations. Visions transmitted and conveyed in the way of FABTE are more acceptable and inspiring to employees.

June Wan was the general manager of a private express company which was in a period of speedy growth due to the rapid development of online shopping business in China. During a quarterly internal meeting he made a speech to his core team members, explaining the vision of his company once again:

Dear colleagues, I think it is necessary for me to spend a bit time talking about the vision of our company one more time. This vision is the result of our repeated discussions and I hope we can keep it deep in our minds. We are in an era of rapid change and I firmly believe that there will be increasing demands for express services due to the emergence of online shopping.

I firmly believe the dream of developing our company into the largest private express enterprise in China and breaking the monopoly of state-owned postal services and foreign logistics giants will come true within ten years. I sincerely hope we can work hard together for the achievement of our common vision. What we are going to achieve will contribute a lot to the development of online shopping and the conveniences of the daily life of Chinese people.

Once our dream comes true, everyone seated here will not only witness and participate in the great changes in our industry, but also be rewarded with large amounts of wealth when our company goes public. None of you will have to worry about the shortage of money for the rest of your life.

Take the two international logistics giants which we are quite familiar for example, their rapid development and expansions were also attributed to the opportunities from industrial reform and change. What's more, some online shopping platforms have just obtained huge investment from venture capitals, which suggests the great potentials and prospects of online shopping. Therefore, I deeply believe that our vision can be realized through our continuous efforts.

From the speech of June Wan, we can clearly discover and find each component of FABTE, details of which are listed in Table 9.3.

The FABTE Mode of Vision Publicity cannot only enable team members to clearly understand the feature and advantage of their team's vision, but also link the personal interests of employees to the future of the whole team through the statement of benefit and trouble (Figure 9.1). What's more, it makes vision more convincing and credible due to the illustration of evidence.

VALUE ROOT

In GE, it was requested that all employees should be equipped with the values of the company. Everyone in GE carried with him or her a card named GE Values. Values of GE were listed on the card and employee's

TABLE 9.3

Sample of FABTE Mode of Vision Publicity

FABTE	FABTE Description	Corresponding Content of June Wan's Speech
Feature	Main feature of the vision	Within ten years, develop our company into the largest private express enterprise in China and break the monopoly of state-owned postal services and foreign logistics giants.
Advantage	Advantages and effects of the vision	Contribute a lot to the development of online shopping and the conveniences of daily life of Chinese people.
Benefit	What benefits can the vision bring to employees	Everyone seated here will not only witness and participate in the great changes in our industry, but also be rewarded with large amounts of wealth when our company goes public.
Trouble	What troubles can the vision help employees get rid of once it is realized?	None of you will have to worry about the shortage of money for the rest of your life.
Evidence	How to prove the feasibility and realizability of the vision?	Take two international logistics giants which we are quite familiar, for example, their rapid development and expansions were also attributed to the opportunities from industrial reform and change. What's more, some online shopping platforms have just obtained huge investment from venture capitals, which suggests the great potentials and prospects of online shopping.

compliance with these values was an indispensable factor determining his or her future promotion.

These values are also major topics of training in the company. Performance evaluations and promotion assessments were done based on interviews by employee's superiors and internal surveys among peers. Although working achievements and conformity to values are both major components of performance evaluation, the latter was attached more importance by top leaders of GE. Jack Welch, former CEO of GE, made it clear that those who have excellent working performance but don't have GE values won't be accepted.

Indirect leaders should be able to implant unified values into the minds of employees. Values of the team must also be turned into codes of conduct

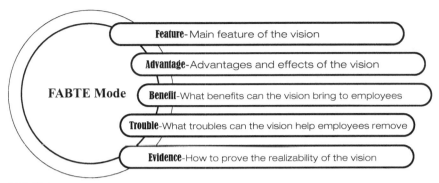

FIGURE 9.1
FABTE mode of vision publicity.

that employees shall comply with. Values are also important weapons that leaders can use to construct psychological contracts between employees and organizations.

Values Are the Roots of Employees' Behaviors

As the size of a team becomes larger and larger, team members will differ from each other in various aspects, such as cultural backgrounds, personal needs and behavioral styles. To guide varieties of employees toward the same direction, leaders should attach much more importance to improving their self-restraint and self-regulation by the values they believe in.

If the performance of an employee is compared to the vitality of a tree, then the achievements leaders want to obtain from employees are similar to the fruits of the tree. The daily behaviors of employees are similar to the branches of the tree and the values believed by employees are analogous to the roots of the tree. Therefore, we call values that are capable of influencing the behaviors and achievements of employees Value Root.

Jack Ma, founder of Alibaba Group, attached great importance to the corporate values of his company. His control of such a huge business empire depended mainly on the values which were deeply rooted in the minds of all of Alibaba's employees. Jack Ma had zero tolerance toward violations of or challenges to the bottom line and authoritativeness of corporate values. He believed that corporate values were the lifelines of Alibaba.

In Alibaba there was an unofficial position called smelling officer who could immediately smell out whether a candidate was suitable for the corporate culture of Alibaba or not. Alibaba released its new corporate values called six meridian swords on September 10, 2019 which was the retirement date of Jack Ma. Although he is no longer the chairman or CEO of the company he founded, his strong influence is ubiquitous in Alibaba because of the values he set.

Jack Ma's MBV (management by values) tells us that leaders who succeed in managing large-scale teams are always good at influencing the whole team through the setting and promotion of values. The inner thinking and daily behaviors of team members are guided and driven by their values. Values are not only the basic codes of conduct for employees to follow but also the reflection of leaders' own behavioral creeds.

Lew Platt, former CEO of HP, used to compare values to the core engine of the effective operation of organizations. John Young, former president of HP, said: "the core values of our company remain unchanged but the ways of handling specific affairs can be changed flexibly."

Regretfully, many leaders fail to transform values of their teams successfully into true value roots. To better influence the inner thinking and daily behaviors of employees, leaders should follow the 3V principles when they are conveying and promoting values of their teams.

3V Principles of the Promotion of Values

The effect of value roots is determined by whether they can exert positive influence on employees' behaviors from inside out. Leaders should follow the 3V principles while transmitting and promoting values in their organizations.

First of all, leaders shall act as the most important mouthpieces, promoters or disseminators of organizational values. They should set good examples to employees by behaving in accordance with values, publicizing values on various occasions and stressing the meaningfulness of values repeatedly. In conclusion, leaders must comply with the first V of the 3V principles, that is, voice of leaders.

Second, leaders shall try to make values tangible and ubiquitous by various visually presenting means, such as symbols, posters, brochures, videos, ceremonies and activities. Values that are abstract and virtual will gradually become ambiguous and fade away. Leaders are also suggested to plan and organize various ceremonies, events and activities so as to ritualize and sanctify values in the minds of employees. In short, leaders must comply with the second V of the 3V principles, that is, visualization.

Finally, employees' adherences to values should be incorporated into their overall performance evaluations. The appraisal of compliance to values can be considered as an important part of employees' overall performance assessments, which refers to the third V of the 3V principles, that is, verification.

Kobe Bryant, the former superstar of the National Basketball Association (NBA), had been nicknamed Mamba which is the most venomous snake on the Africa savannah. The spirit of Kobe—which includes passionate, obsessive, relentless, resilient and fearless—is also called as Mamba Spirit. Kobe, as the leader of his team, was eager to have the Mamba Spirit recognized and shared by other team members.

Actually, the positive impact of Mamba Spirit on other players of the team originated exactly from Kobe's role model effect through his own words and actions. Kobe changed his jersey number from 8 to 24 during the season of 2006–2007.

He once said,

> The number 24 means 24 hours to me and I hope to devote all my time and energy to the sport of basketball. I would not be such a Kobe if I couldn't put all my soul and heart into the game. That's why I choose 24.

Since the change of his jersey number, Kobe got up and started his training at 4:00 a.m. every day. He said he was quite familiar with morning of Los Angeles at 4:00 a.m. Kobe's practice of Mamba Spirit set a good example to and deeply affected others of his team. Mamba spirit was just the values of Kobe's team.

The successful promotion and publicity of Mamba spirit as the value root of the Lakers mainly benefited from Kobe's role model effect through his words and actions, which exhibits the first V of the 3V principles—Voice of Leader.

The promotion of Safety First, one of the values of Du Pont, was very distinctive. Du Pont combined the values of safety with employees' family life through the successful planning and organization of Family Safety Day. Varieties of activities during the Family Safety Day broadened employees' perspectives from safety within working hours at the office to safety any

FIGURE 9.2
3V principles of the promotion of values.

time at home. Hence, employees' understanding of safety first became quite vivid and specified.

Du Pont's promotions of values conformed to the second V of the 3V principles—Visualization. Values should not be abstract and boring in the minds of employees. Values must be vivid, attractive and closely linked to the daily life and work of employees.

Employees' compliances with corporate values are included as an important part into Alibaba's performance evaluation system. Alibaba's top leaders attached great importance to the linkage between employee's abidance by corporate values with their personal interests.

The successful promotion of Alibaba's corporate values contributed greatly to the integration of employees' conformity with values into the overall performance evaluation system, which illustrates the importance of the third V of the 3V principles—Verification (Figure 9.2).

VICTORY CHAIN

Victor graduated from a well-known business school and then joined a multinational enterprise as the general manager of its largest business unit. He found out through investigation that neither new staff nor old employees could achieve their performance objectives set by the company. Based on his previous experience, Victor believed that the objectives set for employees were not quite demanding or unreasonable. He also found that some old staff with long tenure did not stand out from new entrants in terms of working abilities or performances. Meanwhile, almost everyone felt it quite normal and reasonable if he or she failed to achieve performance objectives. No one cared about their results of performance appraisal even if there were punitive measures. After careful deliberation, Victor decided to solve the current problems with the management mode learned from the business school.

First of all, he selected some employees at key positions and held in-depth conversations with them. He made clear to those employees the rationality as well as significance of achieving their performance objectives. In addition, he showed them facts disclosing the higher performance objectives as well as higher ratio of accomplishment of other business units.

After reaching consensus on performance objectives step-by-step with these employees, Victor told them that he had not only expectations on their fulfillment of objectives but also responsibilities for their personal growth and career development.

What's more, he asked everybody to list the skills in urgent need of improvement and set the goals of skill promotion within one year. Through continuous communication and adjustments, Victor reached consensus with those employees on the goals of ability improvement over a one-year term.

In the end, he encouraged them to raise their demands on the support, resources and help from the company which are needed to realize their ability improvement goals. These staff were motivated by the sincerity of Victor and raised various needs and expectations, such as professional training, special tutoring, equipment updating, personnel supply and supportive policies.

Victor evaluated carefully the needs of employees and communicated frankly with them on what needs could be satisfied and why some of the needs weren't able to be met. Final consensus on what Victor can and will do to support the personal growth of these staff were reached.

One week later, a special agreement called the Personal Development Agreement (PDA) was placed on everybody's desk. Both the performance objectives employees were required to achieve and the goals of skill upgrading employees expected to accomplish were specified in the agreement.

Besides, Victor's commitment as the superior to supply all employees with the necessary support, resources and backup for their realization of ability improvement goals was also defined clearly in the PDA. Victor succeeded in having everyone sign their PDAs. Both Victor and these employees promised to honor their own commitments which were stipulated in the agreements.

Almost all of these employees felt greatly motivated and were filled with a sense of responsibility. The PDA contributed a lot to the rapid increase of employees' morale and great improvement of employees' competencies within a short period of time. A year later, all of them accomplished their promised performance objectives.

Generally speaking, both leaders and employees as individuals have the needs as well as desires to attain success. In the workplace, the success of a leader depends mainly on employees' accomplishment of assignments and achievement of performance objectives, while the success of employees depends largely on the improvement of their abilities with the help and support from their leaders.

It is quite usual that leaders set performance objectives for their subordinates from top to bottom and request their commitment to the accomplishment of these objectives. Meanwhile, employees also have their own needs for personal growth and future development as well as hopes for further help and support from their leaders.

An important feature of psychological contract is mutual commitment. Leaders need employee commitment to the accomplishment of their

FIGURE 9.3
Mutual commitments of the victory chain.

TABLE 9.4

Template of Personal Development Agreement

	Performance Objective Description (Highest Objective, Minimum Objective)		
Performance Objectives to be Accomplished	Performance Objective1		
	Performance Objective 2		
	Performance Objective 3		
Ability Improvement Goals to be Achieved	**Ability Improvement Goals**	*Current level of ability*	*Level of ability one year later*
	Goal 1		
	Goal 2		
	Goal 3		
Support Provided by Superiors	**Support from Superiors**	*Description of support*	*Degree of support*
	Support I 1		
	Support 2		
	Support 3		
Commitment from Both Sides	**Party A**: *I promise I will offer all the support listed in this agreement to Party B and help Party B achieve the ability improvement goals.* Signature: **Party B**: *I promise I will try my best to accomplish my performance objectives and ability improvement goals with the support from Party A.* Signature:		

performance objectives and missions assigned to them. In the same way, employees also need the commitment from leaders in offering them the help and support needed for their personal growth and career development. In addition to the mutual promises of economic return in labor contracts, employees and leaders can reach consensus on another kind of mutual commitment in PDA which links the personal growth of employees with the overall performance of the whole team.

Regretfully, many leaders attach much importance to upward commitment (employee's commitment to the achievement of their performance objectives set by leaders) but pay little attention to downward commitment (leaders' commitment to their support of employees' growth and development). Therefore, there is no mutual commitment from both sides and employees will be demotivated for such an unfair mechanism featured by one-way commitment (Figure 9.3). Leaders should combine upward commitment and downward commitment together and specify the commitment of both sides in the PDA. If employees' commitments to the achievement of their performance objectives are compared to one gear of the team's victory chain, then leaders' commitment to the support and growth of employees must be another gear. These two commitment gears interact mutually and work together for the smooth running of the whole victory chain (Table 9.4).

10

Enhancement of the Executive Force of a Team

THREE COMPONENTS OF THE EXECUTIVE FORCE OF A TEAM

It is impossible for indirect leaders of large-scale teams to guide and monitor the behavior of every team member due to the limitation on their time and energy. They should pay more attention to their teams' overall executive force rather than the implementation capability of each individual. The executive force of a team as a whole depends largely on whether there are roadmaps guiding team members toward the right ways and in the correct direction.

Performance Roadmap refers to a set of guidelines, regulations, procedures and standards set by leaders to correct the behaviors as well as improve the performance of employees. With clearly defined performance roadmaps, employees are able to avoid behavioral deviations from expected tracks regardless of whether leaders show them the way in person or not. Performance roadmap can greatly improve employees' understanding of the rules, standards and requirements in their work and provide them with clear navigation of their daily behavior.

The executive force of small teams depends mainly on the personal inspections, supervision and correction from leaders, while the executive force of large-scale teams relies greatly on leaders' abilities of setting, promoting and employing performance roadmaps. In short, the enhancement of employees' personal implementation capabilities can be achieved by face-to-face supervision from leaders, while the improvement of the executive force of the whole team can't be accomplished without performance roadmaps. Once the daily behavior of team members is standardized and guided by effective performance roadmaps, indirect leaders can greatly reduce their time and energy spent on face-to-face inspections, supervision, evaluations and correction.

There are three important tools which can be used in combination by indirect leaders to construct performance roadmaps and improve the executive force of their teams which include Absolute Non-Negotiables (ANN), Standard Execution Procedures (SEP) and Key Responsibility Matrix (KRM). As the acronym of the three tools is ASK, performance roadmap composed of these three major tools is also referred to as the ASK model (Table 10.1).

ANN, SEP and KRM play different roles in the enhancement of the executive force of a team. ANN sets insurmountable prohibition and forbidden areas for the behavior of team members so as to keep everyone on the alert for and away from common mistakes or critical problems which can occur frequently in the early days. SEP specifies and standardizes working procedures as well as operating processes for team members to follow while they are executing assignments. Team members will have clearer courses of action and behavioral standards with the help of SEP. KRM defines and clarifies clearly the powers, responsibilities and interests of related positions or departments when there are conflicts in cross-positional or cross-functional cooperation.

TABLE 10.1

ASK Model of Performance Roadmap

Indirect leaders need to set a few absolutely insurmountable rules (top provisions) which are like high-tension wires to ensure the daily behavior of all team members in safe areas. Anyone who touches the high-tension wires should be severely punished and there is no room for compromise. Although ANN is only a few in number, it helps leaders establish the iron laws of their teams and the bottom lines of the behaviors of team members.

All positions in indirect leaders' teams should be equipped with specified working procedures and standards of execution. SEP not only makes it clear to employees what to do and how to do it, but also clarifies what steps should be followed and what standards should be met. SEP guides as well as restricts the behavior of team members so as to keep their routes of action on the expected track.

Indirect leaders should clearly define the powers, responsibilities and interests of positions or departments involved in cross-positional or cross-functional assignments so as to reduce the phenomena of buck-passing and ambiguous duties. All the related positions or departments should understand and respect the boundary lines of their authorities and responsibilities.

ABSOLUTE NON-NEGOTIABLES

Master Sun's Art *of War* is one of the best-known Chinese classics all over the world. Besides the military arena, the ideas of Master Sun have also been widely applied in fields, such as politics, economics, commerce, diplomacy and sports, making his book a must-read for leaders in these fields.

Sun Tzu was a very famous military commander in China's Spring and Autumn Period. When he came to Wu State, King of Wu treated him as a guest of honor. One day, King of Wu said to him, "Sun Tzu, it is said that you are outstanding in military theories, but I wonder whether you are also good at leading troops in a real war." Sun Tzu answered, "Give me a troop of soldiers, and I'm confident that they can be trained into a distinguished army." "Can you train any group of people into an army?" King of Wu asked again. Sun Tzu replied, "No problem." Then King of Wu pointed at his maids in waiting and said, "Can you train my maids into a strong army?" Sun Tzu said, "As long as you give me enough authorities, I can train all of them into qualified soldiers." "All right, I'll grant you super authorities for six hours," said King of Wu.

Then Sun Tzu asked all of the maids to stand on the training ground. These maids did not take it seriously, just found it so funny and interesting. King of Wu appointed two concubines he loved most as leaders of the two columns of maids. Sun Tzu started his training by shouting at these maids, "Don't talk to each other. Keep silent! I'll count down from 10. When I count to one, everyone must stand in a line and offenders will be beheaded." Instead of listening to him, the maids and imperial concubines just quarreled and laughed but did not move. Sun Tzu shouted at them again,

> You may fail to hear and understand what I have just told you. Now I emphasize a second time that what I have said is a military order that nobody is allowed to violate. I ask all of you to stand in a line immediately.

The female soldiers still remained unresponsive and their laughs continued. Then Sun Tzu said again,

> It may be my fault that I did not make myself understood to you for the first time and second time. Now I'll say it for the third time—I'll count down

from 10 to urge all of you to line up in order, and anybody who fails to do so will be beheaded immediately according to related military regulation.

After Sun Tzu finished his third-time count down, no one followed his command. Sun Tzu became angry and said solemnly, "It may be my fault for the first time and even the second time, but it's your fault for the third time. Now, take away these two team leaders and cut off their heads immediately." At once, these two imperial concubines were arrested. At this moment, King of Wu hastened to say, "Stop doing it! It was just a joke, do not take my word for it."

Sun Tzu said, "Haven't you given me the authority? As the military authority is in my hand, I'll order to behead them immediately." Right after the two imperial concubines were beheaded, all the maids were shocked and then lined up at once. These two concubines were beheaded because they took the lead in violating the ANN set by Sun Tzu for the team. ANN is viewed as the negative list, which is the insurmountable bottom line set by leaders to guard against negative and destructive behaviors of team members.

ANN are the core rules that leaders request all of their team members to abide by. They are the high-voltage cables that everyone must avoid and the forbidden zone that nobody can touch. Whoever overrides ANN must be punished without exception.

Three Types of Absolute Non-Negotiables

We can classify various ANN into three categories, which include violation of core policies or regulations, violation of ethics or moral restraints and failure to meet minimum performance requirements.

Sun Tzu sentenced the king's concubines to death because they didn't obey the military orders from him. Sun Tzu's ANN set for these female soldiers can be classified as the first type, that is, violation of core policies or regulations. Leaders should turn policies or regulations that are most likely to be ignored or violated by employees into ANN.

In 2011, Alibaba's B2B Company announced that the Board of Directors had approved the request from Wei Zhe to resign from his position as its CEO. Jack Ma, chairman of the Board of Directors of Alibaba, sent an internal e-mail to all his employees and claimed,

Over the past month, I have been quite painful, irritant and angry. Any tolerance of behaviors violating business integrity and the bottom line of our company would be considered as a crime against creditable clients and honest employees of Alibaba.

The e-mail sent by Jack Ma to his internal employees was in fact a letter to the public media. Jack Ma said that the management team led by Wei Zhe was responsible for the alleged fraud of Alibaba's 1,107 Chinese suppliers against overseas clients. Jack Ma stressed repeatedly that anyone who was found dishonest or conniving through dishonest behavior would be severely punished. The behaviors of Wei Zhe and his management team violated one of the ANN set by Jack Ma for Alibaba employees, that is, dishonest behavior or connivance through dishonest behavior are strictly prohibited. The top executives of Alibaba B2B company who tolerated and fostered dishonest behaviors did not comply with the second type of ANN—violation of ethics or moral rules. Leaders should list ethics or moral rules which are frequently breached by employees as ANN.

Felix was the general manager of a well-known listed company which was in a period of steady growth. Many middle and grassroots managers who had worked in the company for many years lost passion and enthusiasm for their jobs gradually. After trying many incentive methods with no results, Felix employed a renowned consulting firm to design a new performance evaluation system for middle and grassroots managers. The new appraisal system was composed of four performance indicators which include indicator of outcome, indicator of growth, indicator of behavior and indicator of competitiveness. The average score of evaluation of all these indicators would be calculated and released on a periodical basis.

Felix officially announced to all employees that the person with the lowest annual performance evaluation would be fired. His new measures of performance management were aimed at reducing the number of employees who failed to reach their basic performance expectations, which can be classified into the third type of ANN—failure to reach the minimum performance requirements. Table 10.2 can be referred to by leaders as a template when they are setting ANN for their teams.

TABLE 10.2

Formulation of Three Types of Absolute Non-Negotiables

Three Types of ANN	Stipulations Included	Punitive Measures
Violation of core policies or regulations		
Violation of ethics or moral rules		
Failure to meet minimum performance requirements		

Five Major Characteristics of Effective Absolute Non-Negotiables

Ironically, although almost all kinds of organizations have varieties of disciplines and regulations, many of these disciplines and regulations exist in name only. ANN has greater deterrence and more influence on employees' behavior than ordinary disciplines and regulations because of the following features (Figure 10.1).

The first characteristic of ANN is universality, which means that ANN only addresses common problems or frequently committed errors. Personalized problems and mistakes can be handled and corrected by leaders one-on-one. As to universal problems, indirect leaders need to add them onto the list of ANN so that everyone in the team can be warned against and stay alert to them.

ANN are always few in number, thus, they can be widely known and deeply rooted in the minds of employees. The quantity of ANN is usually no more than five. Few in number is the second characteristic of ANN. Clear definition is the third characteristic of ANN. ANN should not be blurred, abstract or ambiguous. In contrast, it should be quite clear, definite and well-circumscribed. In fact, the disciplines and regulations of many organizations are lack of deterrence because of their unclear definitions on right or wrong and poor distinctions between compliance and breach.

The fourth characteristic of ANN is immediate punishment. Those who violate ANN will be punished immediately without exception. The Hot Stove Principle tells us that anyone who touches a hot stove is bound to get burned. ANN conform to the Hot Stove Principle and none of the

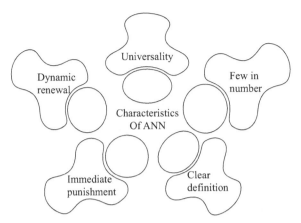

FIGURE 10.1
Characteristics of Absolutely Non-Negotiables.

offenders has immunity, even leaders themselves. ANN are just like the Swords of Damocles which keep warning against destructive behaviors.

The fifth characteristic of ANN is dynamic renewal. ANN are not fixed and unchanged. They have to be renewed and replaced every three months. After three months, when the problems or mistakes of corresponding ANN disappear, these ANNs should be deleted from the list and replaced by new ANNs once there emerge new problems or errors. ANN have stronger timeliness and pertinence than ordinary disciplines or regulations.

STANDARD EXECUTION PROCEDURES

To regulate and normalize the daily behavior of team members, indirect leaders should no longer depend on one-on-one examination, evaluation and supervision. They should spend more time on the simplification of complex work assignments and standardization of ambiguous operating procedures in order to improve the executive force of their teams as a whole.

SEP is such a management tool that leaders can employ for the sake of standardizing, simplifying and specifying the job specification and task description for team members. Key positions or important tasks ought to be equipped with standardized steps of implementation and operating procedures so as to reduce errors and guard against undesirable consequences. Hence SEP is aimed at promoting performance through improvement of process management.

Take driving a car for example. In order to help employees drive correctly and arrive at their expected destinations on time, leaders can choose to adopt two types of management modes. In mode 1, leaders have to sit next to their employees inside the car, showing them the right way and correcting deviations resulted from their operating errors. However, leaders won't have enough time and energy to adopt mode 1 when they are leading a large number of employees. In mode 2, leaders choose to install navigation systems such as GPS in all the cars of employees. As along as every employee follows the guidance of the navigation system, he or she is more likely to drive properly and succeed in arriving at the destination on time. Navigation system is just an analogy of SEP set by leaders for their team members.

SEP is effective and productive for large-scale teams no matter how many members there are. If SEP is strictly followed by all employees, everything will remain well-regulated and in order even if leaders say or do nothing. SEP contributes a lot to the realization of indirect management and improves the overall executive force of teams because:

1. SEP can help leaders relieve their management pressures dramatically, freeing them from a lot of hands-on guidance, coaching and supervision.
2. SEP enables employees to clearly understand their job specifications as well as the performance expectations from leaders. Performance deviations of employees result partly from the gap between their own understanding of what to do and their leaders' expectations of what they should do. SEP is an effective way to narrow such a gap and correct performance deviations.
3. SEP produces process indicators for the performance evaluation of employees in addition to outcome indicators. In particular, process control with the help of SEP is indispensable to the accomplishment of expected results for long-cycle assignments, programs or projects.

Upgrade SEP by Fixing Six Types of Bugs

Generally speaking, all the key positions of any mature organization ought to have their corresponding SEPs. However, indirect leaders should still diagnose whether there are vulnerabilities or deficiencies in the existing SEPs by paying close attention to the following phenomena:

1. Phenomenon 1: There are still varieties of problems and continuous deviations occurring in the process of execution even if employees follow corresponding SEPs which already exist. Leaders should try to find out whether such a Phenomenon results from the vulnerabilities or imperfections of existing SEPs. The need to upgrade and perfect the current SEPs should be considered by leaders.
2. Phenomenon 2: As there are changes taking place constantly, leaders should analyze whether the existing SEPs have lagged behind and are unable to keep up with changes. Actions ought to be taken by leaders to improve and optimize the existing SEPs so that they can fit better with new situations.

Indirect leaders need to develop themselves into systematic thinkers. Any problem, mistake or error should be considered as a bug in the existing system, so that leaders can solve it once and for all by focusing on the repairment and perfection of corresponding SEPs.

During World War I, the allied force of Britain and America launched a large-scale bombing on Germany. Due to the strong defensive power of Germany, the allied air force suffered huge losses, with lots of aircrafts crashing and the death rate of pilots close to 11%. A research team led by Tomson was founded in order to improve the protective capabilities of airplanes. Tomson and his assistants examined all the airplanes returning from their missions, discovering that the bellies of these airplanes were covered with bullet marks while the wings stayed intact.

Therefore, Tomson and his team devoted all their efforts to the reinforcement of the belly of aircraft. They perfected the manufacturing technology and used more solid manufacturing materials. However, the rate of air crash and pilot death had not declined. Just when Tomson was at a loss, a friend called to remind him:

Have you worked in the wrong direction? Those aircrafts that were hit by bullets in their bellies returned successfully, while those that were hit on their wings crashed. Therefore, what you should strengthen and consolidate is not the bellies but the wings of aircrafts.

Tomson was suddenly enlightened. He began his work by focusing on the consolidation and optimization of the wings and then great progress was made. As a result, the crash rate of airplanes with consolidated wings was greatly reduced. What leaders can learn from this story is that they should solve problems thoroughly by diagnosing the bugs of existing systems and repairing existing SEPs. What seems to be right may be quite wrong if leaders think from systematic perspectives.

Any leader with systematic thinking shall learn to diagnose and fix six types of systematic bugs which include new changes difficult to adapt to, complicated tasks easily done wrong, repeated mistakes hard to be corrected, unexpected emergencies that needed to be prevented, common misunderstandings to be eliminated and fragmented experience difficult to be duplicated. All these systematic bugs should be successfully discovered by leaders and fixed through upgrading corresponding SEPs (Table 10.3).

These above-mentioned systematic bugs should be examined and diagnosed regularly in order to further improve and upgrade existing SEPs. An aircraft of Xiamen Airline failed to have its landing chassis retrieved because a critical bolt was unable to be pulled out. Although no serious damage was caused, the management team of Xiamen Airline still attached great importance to such an accident. The CEO of Xiamen Airline pointed out that the fault of bolt-pulling would lead to disasters and should be corrected thoroughly by standardizing the operating procedures.

According to the new SEP formulated for bolt-polling, the ground crew must walk 15 steps back after pulling out the latches. Meanwhile, they should keep holding up their hands until the pilot sends signals allowing them to put hands down. It was also stipulated that when there was repairment being conducted under the fuselage, a two-meter-long red ribbon would be floated up as a signal to prevent any operation of the airplane.

Ever since the bolt-pulling accident, leaders of Xiamen Airline realized deeply the significance of SEP to the improvement of daily management and the promotion of employees' execution. Gradually SEP as an important management practice was promoted by Xiamen Airline to other fields of safety management and tremendous improvements were made.

Leaders at Xiamen Airline were systematic thinkers. In their minds, there were still hidden dangers to be eliminated although the accident was successfully handled. Only by diagnosing the systematic bugs and perfecting the SEP can problems be solved once and for all. According to the six types

TABLE 10.3

Six Types of Bugs to be Fixed through Upgrading SEP

Six Types of Bugs	Definition
New changes difficult to adapt to	Leaders should evaluate whether there are some new and recent changes which make the existing SEPs outdated. SEPs have to be updated and upgraded so as to fit with new changes.
Complicated tasks easy to be done wrongly	Leaders must find out whether there are some assignments which are too complicated and confusing for employees to understand and implement clearly. SEPs should be set by leaders for these assignments so as to make the implementation of them more specified, simplified and standardized.
Repeated mistakes hard to be corrected	Leaders need to diagnose whether there are some mistakes or errors that occur frequently and repeatedly. These mistakes and errors are probably resulted from deficiencies in the existing SEPs.
Unexpected emergencies that need to be prevented	Leaders have to evaluate whether there have been some emergencies with severe consequences recently. If these emergencies are originated from vulnerabilities in current SEPs, leaders should prevent them from taking place again by perfecting and improving the existing SEPs.
Common misunderstandings to be eliminated	Leaders should examine whether there are some existing SEPs toward which a majority of employees have misunderstanding or incomprehension. These SEPs must have hidden defects to be repaired and corrected by leaders.
Fragmented experience unable to be duplicated	Leaders need to find out whether there is personal working experience of some employees unable to be duplicated and mastered by others. Such fragmented personal experience should be transformed into SEPs so that they can be easily duplicated inside the team and shared by all the members.

of bugs, the misconduct of bolt-pulling in this case can be categorized as the bug of unexpected emergencies needed to be prevented.

Three Key Features of Effective SEP

Leaders can greatly improve employees' effectiveness of execution by formulating SEPs for key positions or important missions. An effective SEP

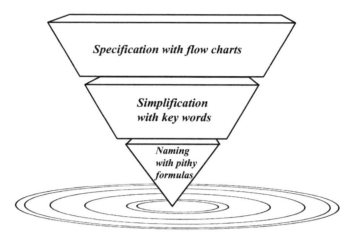

FIGURE 10.2
Features of effective SEPs.

usually has three key features, which are specification with flow charts, simplification with key words and naming with pithy formula.

Effective SEPs are always presented in the form of flow charts so as to visually present the sequences, steps and logical structures of working processes. Graphics are much clearer, more visualized and easier to be remembered than words. Specification with flow charts is the first feature of effective SEPs, which ought to be born in the minds of leaders.

Leaders need to condense the complicated descriptions of behavioral standards or working processes into simplified keywords or key phrases. The more simplified descriptions of SEPs are, the clearer employee's understanding will be. It's a pity that many leaders are unaware of the significance of the second feature of effective SEP: simplification with key words. Leaders can name the SEP they have set with rhymes or pithy formulas, making SEP easier to be remembered, understood and spread by employees. For example, the phrase of Keep It Simple and Specified can be condensed as the key word of KISS. Naming with pithy formula is the third characteristic of highly effective SEPs (Figure 10.2).

Specification with Flow Charts

In order to make the logical relationships between each step of SEPs clearer, leaders need to exhibit the internal structures of SEPs with flow charts.

There are three distinctive advantages if an SEP is shown in the form of flow charts:

1. The logical relationship between all the steps of the SEP is quite clear when shown in the form of flow charts, which is quite helpful to employees' understanding and mastery of the SEP.
2. Flow charts can help new staff quickly master related working procedures and behavioral standards and greatly shorten their learning cycles.
3. By drawing the flow charts of SEPs, leaders can find out the deficiencies and problems in current working procedures and take corrective action in time.

Basically, there are eight types of graphics which can be used by leaders to draw the flow charts of SEPs (Table 10.4).

TABLE 10.4

Eight Types of Graphics in Flow Charts

Graphics	Definition	Specific Meaning
	(Start)	Start the flow chart
	(Processing)	Process procedures
	(Decision)	Choose from different solutions
	(End)	Terminate the flow chart
	(Path)	Show the direction of path
	(Document)	Input or output of documents
	(Predefined Processing)	Use a predefined processing procedure
	(Connector)	Connect one flow chart to another one
	(Comment)	Make explanatory notes

Simplification with Key Words

It is better for leaders to summarize the descriptions of each critical step of SEP into simplified and clear key words or key phrases. Simplification with key words can help employees quickly understand and memorize what they are expected to accomplish. It may be a kind of ability if leaders are able to make simple things complicated, but it must be higher-level abilities of leaders if they can convert complexity into simplification.

Grassroots employees will feel it annoying and even boring when they are asked to understand and follow SEPs that are described in complicated and fragmented detail. Therefore, if leaders can turn complicated and fragmented descriptions into simplified key words or key phrases, the understanding, recognition and acceptances of employees will be greatly improved.

There are many great leaders who are good at simplification. They are able to help employees generalize and refine key points of their work and transform them into working processes which are composed of key words or key phrases.

Edison, the training and development director of a well-known company, found that those internal trainers who were responsible for delivering technical training to grassroots employees differed from each other in terms of training styles. Some trainers were used to cutting to the chase in their training but their lecturing was unattractive and even boring. Some trainers loved story-telling but their training content always deviated from the topic. While some other trainers were good starters but poor finishers, failing to offer useful solutions to problems grassroots employees encountered. Edison felt it was better for him to formulate a standardized training procedure for these internal trainers rather than offering one-on-one coaching to them. He succeeded in setting a six-step training procedure for grassroots employees and asked his internal trainers to prepare and deliver their training based on the procedure. Details of the procedure are shown in Table 10.5.

From Table 10.5 we can see that Edison succeeded in specifying the steps of the training procedure and setting clear requirements for each step. However, Edison thought this six-step procedure was not perfect because the description of each step had not been summarized and condensed into simplified key words. In Table 10.6, Edison highly refined and generalized each step of the training procedure into six key words so as to make this SEP more memorable and impressive.

TABLE 10.5

Six-step Training Procedure for Grassroots Employees

Six Steps	Detailed Requirements
Step 1	Prepare and present attractive opening of training in various forms such as story-telling, case study, ice-breaking game, video-showing or group discussion so as to make the training topic more appealing.
Step 2	Introduce and elaborate the topic as well as learning objectives of training, so that training participants can quickly understand what is going to be taught.
Step 3	Point out the main problems and repeated mistakes among employees regarding the topic of this training.
Step 4	Share practical methods and effective solutions with participants pertaining to the above-mentioned problems.
Step 5	Remind employees of some issues that they should pay attention to while these shared solutions are applied in real situation.
Step 6	List specific post-training actions for the training participants.

TABLE 10.6

Refined Six-step Training Procedure for Grassroots Employees

Steps	Key Word	Detailed Requirements
Step 1	Trigger	Prepare and present attractive opening of training in various forms, such as story-telling, case study, ice-breaking game, video-showing or group discussion so as to make the training topic more appealing.
Step 2	Topic	Introduce and elaborate the topic as well as learning objectives of training, so that training participants can quickly understand what is going to be taught.
Step 3	Problem	Point out the main problems and repeated mistakes among employees regarding the topic of this training.
Step 4	Solution	Share practical methods and effective solutions with participants pertaining to the above-mentioned problems.
Step 5	Attention	Remind employees of some issues that they should pay attention to while these shared solutions are applied in real situations.
Step 6	Action	List specific post-training actions for the training participants.

Naming with Pithy Formulas

Leaders should also name the SEP in an easy-to-read and easy-to-understand way. SEPs will be memorable, unforgettable and should be easily spread by word of mouth if their names can impress on employees deeply and create visual imaginations in their minds.

For example, if a SEP set for customer service improvement is composed of four steps, it is better for leaders to name it as four driving wheels of effective customer service than to name it as four steps of effective customer service. If a SEP for quality reexamination is made up of five steps, five firewalls of quality reexamination is a much better name than five key points of quality reexamination. If a SEP for technical innovation contains six steps, six levers of technical innovation as the name is better than six components of technical innovation. In addition to naming SEP in a way of number plus visualized object, leaders can also use acronyms to name SEP. For example, ANN, SEP and KRM forms the ASK mode of the team's overall executive force.

Luis, director of the maintenance department of a manufacturing company, summarized the daily work of maintenance into a four-step procedure for engineers to follow. What's more, he refined and condensed the specific requirements of each step into four key words which include Check, Action, Share and Handle. Finally, he succeeded in naming the process as CASH using the acronym of these four words.

KEY RESPONSIBILITY MATRIX

ANN is aimed at making all team members clear about what they cannot do. SEP is targeted at making team members clear about what they should do and how they should do it, while a KAM is focused on making team members clear about their authorities and responsibilities when they are cooperating with others.

Many problems related to the execution of large-size teams originate from unclear authorities as well as responsibilities of positions involved in collaborative assignments. There may be different people who are nominally responsible for the same job but nobody actually takes accountability. It is impossible for leaders of large-scale teams to handle conflicts between employees with collaborative relationships one by one. Therefore, indirect leaders need to make authorities as well as responsibilities clear enough to these employees so as to minimize the possibility of conflicts.

Almost all leaders are eager to build a sense of duty in the minds of their employees which is critical to the improvement of the executive force of their teams. But sense of duty in the minds of employees will be baseless if there is no mechanism of duty in the organization. KRM is such a mechanism that defines clearly the responsibilities, authorities and interests of employees with collaborative relationships, which enables leaders to let the sun shine through in the chaotic and grey areas.

Three Major Components of Key Responsibility Matrix

KRM is a management tool that indirect leaders can use to clearly define and specify the responsibilities and duties of positions or departments with collaborative relationships. In the template of KAM (Table 10.7) shown below, leaders can see that listed in the vertical column at the left side of the table are jobs or tasks be done, while listed in the horizontal column along the top of the table are the positions involved in these jobs or tasks. The authority and responsibility (A&R) of each position corresponding to each related task is listed and presented in the intersecting grids.

From the template of KRM shown above, it is not difficult for leaders to recognize three main advantages of KRM which are listed as follows:

- Make staff with collaborative relationships clearly understand their authorities and responsibilities so as to lower the possibility of buck-passing resulted from unclear A&R.
- Help staff with collaborative relationships know clearly who they are cooperating with and which departments they are coordinating with. Further, staff should also know who they can turn to for assistance if problems arise.
- Make it clear to staff with collaborative relationships what they are allowed to do and what they are prohibited from doing in the process of accomplishing tasks.

TABLE 10.7

Template of Key Responsibility Matrix

Position Task	Position A	Position B	Position C	Position D
Task A	A & R	A & R	A & R	A & R
Task B	A & R	A & R	A & R	A & R
Task C	A & R	A & R	A & R	A & R
Task D	A & R	A & R	A & R	A & R
Task E	A & R	A & R	A & R	A & R

TABLE 10.8

Key Responsibility Matrix of the After-sales Service Affairs

Position Task	Customer Service Specialist	After-sale Service Director	After-sale Service Secretary	Service Engineer	Maintenance Engineer	Product Engineer
Customer reception	R			I	I	I
Record errors	R					
Fill in maintenance form	R	A				
Assign task		A				
Diagnose and repair	I			R	I	I
Send service form to customer			I	R		
Record and file documents			R	R		
Follow-up service	R			R	I	I
Explanation of A, R and I	A: Approval and decision-making R: Direct and main responsibilities I: Involvement and secondary responsibilities.					

Table 10.8 is an example of KAM for affairs of after-sales service. Tasks such as customer reception, fault recording and follow-up service are listed vertically at the left side of the table, while shown horizontally along top of the table are six positions involved in affairs of after-sales service, such as customer service specialist, after-sale service director, and so on. In the intersections of the table, there are the authorities and responsibilities of each position. The descriptions of authorities and responsibilities of different positions in this KAM table are simplified into three letters which are A, R and I.

Six Major Steps of Formulating KRM

Leaders should be responsible for the formulation and promotion of KAMs inside their teams and make KAMs widely accepted and recognized by all employees.

TABLE 10.9

Six Major Steps of Formulating KRM

Six Major Steps	Specific Requirements
Step 1: Define and specify the tasks to be accomplished	First of all, indirect leaders shall define and specify all the tasks needed to be accomplished. These tasks are interrelated but remain independent from each other. Tasks are listed in the vertical columns at the left side of the KAM table.
Step 2: Identify and list the positions involved	Indirect leaders should also identify all the positions involved in the accomplishment of tasks and list them in the horizontal columns on top of the KAM table.
Step 3: Draft the table of KAM	Based on the tasks listed vertically and positions listed horizontally, leaders can finish the drafting of KRM tables.
Step 4: Make clear authorities and responsibilities	Responsibilities and authorities of different positions for corresponding tasks should be clearly defined and presented in intersecting grids of the table. Letters, symbols, numbers or other forms can be used to refer to the authorities and responsibilities. Leaders can also use text to describe A&R in details.
Step 5: Adjust and optimize	Leaders discuss with all the parties involved and further improve the draft KAMs based on the opinions and suggestions collected.
Step 6: Get confirmation and commitment from employees	Leaders send the finalized version of KRM to everyone involved and ask for his or her confirmation as well as commitment.

Moreover, they need to listen to the opinions and feedback from positions involved so as to further improve and optimize the KAMs. Finally, leaders need to ensure that employees working at positions involved in collaborative assignments can make commitments to the agreed KRMs. To make KAMs more effective, leaders are suggested to follow six key steps shown in Table 10.9 when they are formulating and promoting KRMs.

Leaders can describe the A&R of related positions in two ways. It is better for leaders to use simple letters or other symbols to represent authorities and responsibilities so as to make A&R easier to be recognized and understood. When authorities and responsibilities are explained clearly and briefly, descriptions can then be adopted in word form. In addition, when descriptions of authorities and responsibilities cannot be represented with letters or other symbols, description in words is still needed. Symbols such as letters are widely used to refer to authorities and responsibilities because of their simplicity, explicitness and standardization.

11

Enhancement of the Cohesive Force of a Team

INTERPERSONAL SYNERGY QUOTIENT OF A TEAM

In June 2004, Los Angeles Lakers played against Detroit Pistons in the finals of NBA. Few people believed that Detroit Pistons would make it to the seventh section because LA Lakers at that time was considered as a super team. LA Lakers was composed of various super stars who were almost the best in the league for every position. In the eyes of many people, this was the strongest team in the history of NBA over 20 years. There was only a theoretical possibility of defeating them in the finals, let alone Detroit Pistons being only a civilian team without super stars.

The result, however, was beyond the expectations of most people as the Lakers were soon defeated by a total score of 1:4. The failure was rooted mainly in the inadequate cohesiveness of the team. Both O'Neal and Kobe considered themselves as the real leader of the team. Therefore, they fought alone in the game without enough collaboration with each other. Malone and Payton, who only came for the NBA championship rings, could not integrate themselves into the whole team and give maximum effort to their roles. It was disunity and lack of cohesiveness that led to the miserable failure of the Lakers.

Leaders can learn from this case that the whole team will probably become mediocre if there are frictions and conflicts between outstanding individuals. Under this circumstance, the result of one plus one will not be bigger than two, or even smaller than two. While building and developing their teams, lots of leaders tend to find the best individuals who are competent enough for their positions. However, if these excellent talents cannot cooperate with each other complementarily and effectively, their resultant force will be even less than that of a team composed of mediocre individuals who possess the spirit of teamwork.

There was an experiment which was aimed at testing the tensile force of people. First, one man was asked to pull the rope at full stretch and his strength was measured and recorded. Then two men were asked to pull the same rope as hard as they could. Their joint force was measured and divided by two. The average force of each man was 95% of that of the first man who pulled the rope by himself.

Then three men were asked to pull the same rope with their full force. The pulling force produced by them was calculated and divided by three. The averaged force of each man was only 85% of that of the first man. Finally, eight men were asked to pull the rope with full might. The averaged pulling force was only 49% of that of the first man.

This experiment tells us that when a team expands to a certain size, there will emerge internal frictions and interpersonal conflicts between members while they are making contribution to their team. The larger the size of a team is, the more severe the internal frictions and the less the resultant force will be.

A large number of cases in the workplace show that the ability improvement of individuals in a team will not necessarily bring about the improvement of the team's overall competitiveness and performance. Also, excellence of individuals does not necessarily mean excellence of the whole team. The bigger the scale of a team, the lower mutual trust between team members will be and the weaker the team's cohesiveness will become. Therefore, indirect leaders managing teams with a large number of members should upgrade from developing the competences of individuals to improving the overall performance of the whole team.

As a Chinese saying goes, one boy is a boy, two boys are equal to half a boy, three boys are equivalent to none. The team composed of three boys has huge internal frictions and distrust, making it less capable and less productive than an individual. Another nursery rhyme chants, one ant carrying rice cannot make it, however hard it tries, two ants carrying rice make it possible with their bodies shaking back and forth, and three ants carry rice easily into the cave with their joint efforts. Due to high degree of cohesiveness, these three ants can accomplish the task effortlessly.

We usually evaluate the talent or character of an individual by Intelligence Quotient (IQ), Emotional Quotient (EQ), Daring Quotient (DQ), and so on. Likewise, we can measure the overall cohesiveness of a team by interpersonal Synergy Quotient (ISQ), which refers to the degree of interpersonal synergy and mutual trust between members of a team. From the perspective of ISQ, the whole team is regarded as an individual and the level of smooth communication and harmonious interaction between team members shall be appraised and examined.

The level of ISQ of all kinds of large teams can be measured by seven indicators, which are specified as follows:

Members Show High Willingness to Accept the Final Decision of Their Team

Team members highly recognize the advantages and necessities of decisions made by team leaders. Even if they do not agree with some of the decisions, they will still choose to accept and implement them.

Once a decision is made, team members are willing to give up their own interests and show respect to the consensus reached by most members. If there are still different opinions, team members will leave them to the next group discussion instead of resisting passively or even opposing openly.

Members Are Quite Willing to Cooperate with Others

Team members are always ready to cooperate with people both inside and outside their team. Even if they can achieve higher efficiency by working independently sometimes, team members are still willing to work together with others for the long-term interests of their team. Team members are willing to share knowledge, experience and resources with others, so that other members can also improve their working efficiency and effectiveness.

Members Show Enough Respect to the Personal Interests of Others

Members of a team with high ISQ are compassionate and considerate. They always show their understanding toward others and respect the personal interests of other members.

When there are conflicts and contradictions, team members will communicate and coordinate effectively with others to find win–win solutions instead of fighting for their own interests at the sacrifice of interpersonal synergy of the team.

Members Recognize and Appreciate the Contribution of Others

Each member of a team with high ISQ is used to recognizing and appreciating the contribution of other members to the team. Everyone regards himself or herself as an important part of the whole team. He or she will not claim credit for himself or herself while faced with achievements. On the contrary, he or she will attribute the achievements to the joint efforts of the whole team and to the support from other members.

Members Offer Constructive Suggestions and Criticisms

For the overall and long-term interests of the team, members will actively share with others their own opinions and viewpoints. What's more, they will be open-minded in raising suggestions as well as criticisms to any problems which are harmful to the whole team. These suggestions and criticisms are always constructive and positive without hurting the feelings of others.

Members Assume Responsibilities of Solving Problems Proactively

In a team with high ISQ, members have a strong sense of responsibility and are willing to share the duties of others. Team members build trust with each other during the process of mutual assistance. While faced with problems or troubles, team members will never put the blame on each other but assume the responsibilities of solving problem proactively.

There Are No Antagonistic or Destructive Informal Groups in the Team

There will be no destructive informal groups in teams with high ISQ. Even if there are some informal groups in such teams, these groups are constructive and helpful to the harmony, trust and cooperation between team members. What can indirect leaders do to promote the ISQ and cohesive force of their teams? Are there any applicable strategies and ways of enhancing the harmony, trust and cooperation between team members?

TABLE 11.1

FIT Mode of Cohesiveness Enhancement

FIT	Specific Description
Fellowship with Complementary Roles	The cohesiveness of a team is largely determined by whether the roles of team members are complementary to each other or not. If members are playing complementary roles in the team, there will be high level of harmony and mutual trust between them. On the contrary, if members are playing conflicting roles, the cohesiveness of the team will be baseless and easy to destroy.
Informal Group Alliance	There must be various types of informal groups in large-scale teams. Members of these groups are united around informal leaders. Therefore, leaders shall not only reduce the antagonism and destructiveness of these informal groups but also ally with them in different ways to promote the cohesiveness of their teams.
Trust Circle Building	Leaders should build trust circles with core staff as initial members and expand trust circles step by step with more qualified members joining in. Leaders can enhance the mutual trust between members of the trust circle by setting up and reinforcing varieties of trust bonds.

If the word FIT refers to the harmonious coexistence and friendly cooperation between team members, then there happen to be three major tools of cohesion improvement with their English phrases starting from F, I and T. These three tools are fellowship with complementary roles, informal group alliance and trust circle building, which are named as the FIT mode of cohesiveness enhancement and are described in Table 11.1.

FELLOWSHIP WITH COMPLEMENTARY ROLES

Leaders always have high expectation of the excellence of their team members. An important indicator measuring the excellence of employees is post competency, that is, whether an employee is competent and qualified enough for his or her own position.

However, post competency merely evaluates the performance of employees from the perspective of individuals but not the team as a whole, thus it does not necessarily reflect the real contribution made by employees to their teams. Sometimes the contribution made by highly competent employees to their teams is much less than that of those seemingly mediocre employees due to their frequent conflicts and contradictions with other members.

Therefore, indirect leaders shall not only evaluate their employees from the perspective of post competency, but also appraise them from the perspective of team roles. As soon as an employee joins the team, he or she will no longer be an individual but play one or several roles in the team.

Seven Major Roles in a Team

In the eyes of Chinese people, there are in total seven basic colors making up the whole color spectrum, which are red, orange, yellow, green, cyan, blue and purple. As far as team roles are concerned, there are also seven roles played by employees in a team which are named after these seven colors (see Figure 11.1). The contribution, advantages and shortcomings of these seven roles are listed and shown in the following table (Table 11.2).

Promote Cohesiveness by Perfecting the Composition of Team Roles

Teams which have balanced composition of these seven roles will be more competitive in terms of cohesive force. The role of cyan is good at

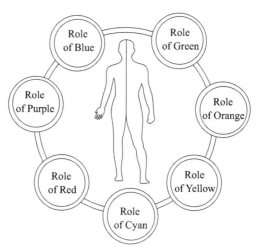

FIGURE 11.1
Seven major roles in a team.

TABLE 11.2

Seven Major Roles in a Team

Seven Roles	Contribution, Advantages and Shortcomings of Roles
Role of Blue	• Contribution: Responsible for carrying out challenging assignments and difficult jobs of the team and always ready to share the workloads of other members • Advantages: Diligent, hardworking, self-disciplined and accommodating • Shortcomings: Not flexible and innovative in the process of execution
Role of Orange	• Contribution: Responsible for assigning appropriate tasks and resources to the most suitable people of the team • Advantages: Skillful in defining assignments and identifying the most qualified team members to implement them • Shortcomings: Unwilling to doing things by himself or herself
Role of Cyan	• Contribution: Responsible for breaking the routine and finding innovative solutions when team members encounter problems or troubles • Advantages: Intelligent, imaginative, creative and independent in thinking • Shortcomings: Too arrogant and lack of respect to others' suggestions and ideas
Role of Yellow	• Contribution: Responsible for urging others to perform correctly and quickly as well as monitoring the behaviors of others • Advantages: Particular about progress and efficiency in implementation, willing to remind others of their duties and conscientious • Shortcomings: Not good at motivating and encouraging others and too pushy
Role of Red	• Contribution: Responsible for interfering in team members' contractions and conflicts and devoted to reconciliating contradictions and quieting down conflicts • Advantages: Skilled in interpersonal relationship improvement and adept at building trust • Shortcomings: Hesitant and easy to give up in serious conflicts
Role of Green	• Contribution: Responsible for formulating detailed implementation plans and course of actions for team members • Advantages: Rational and logical in thinking; and skilled in turning ideas into plans • Shortcomings: Unaware of the timing of implementation while pursuing the perfection of his or her action plan
Role of Purple	• Contribution: Responsible for searching for as well integrating various support and resources from outside to better solve the problems team members are faced with. • Advantages: Sensitive to changes outside the team, excellent in negotiation and good at finding resources from various channels • Shortcomings: Neglectful to existing resources inside the team

proposing innovative solutions, the role of purple is able to explore and exploit useful resources from outside, the role of orange is experienced in matching team members with suitable tasks, the role of green is skilled in formulating detailed action plans, the role of yellow is willing to remind others of their progress, the role of red is responsible for solving conflicts and the role of blue is a determined executor.

Each of these seven roles is indispensable and the absence of any role will have negative impacts on the cohesiveness of the team.

- Without the role of blue, many ideas and plans cannot be put into practice no matter how good they are. Conflicts may emerge as nobody is willing to take responsibilities and have tough jobs done.
- Without the role of orange, many tasks are assigned to inappropriate people and conflicts may emerge as team members always complain that they have to do what they are not good at.
- If the role of cyan does not exist, team members won't be able to come up with creative solutions and ideas when they are faced with problems or troubles.
- If the role of purple does not exist, conflict may emerge as team members have to compete for limited resources inside the team.
- Without the role of green, team members will probably fail to achieve expected results because they don't have clear action plans and behavioral guidance.
- Interpersonal synergy and mutual trust between team members will be lowered greatly if the role of red does not exist.
- Without the role of yellow, there is no one in the team who will remind others of their performance gaps and warn them against possible risks.

While building teams and choosing members, indirect leaders shall try to think from the perspective of team roles and solve problems through supplementing the missing roles. For example, if leaders find that the level of interpersonal harmony is low in their teams, then the role of red should be added or strengthened. If there are increasing problems or challenges that make team members at a loss, then the role of cyan and green need to be supplemented. If most team members are undisciplined and irresponsible, there should be more yellow roles in the team (Tables 11.3 and 11.4).

TABLE 11.3

Self-evaluation Table of Your Roles

Test Form of Team Roles

There are six questions to be answered by you and each one has seven statements. Please distribute ten points to these seven statements. The rule of distribution is that the statement that can best reflect your behavior gets the highest score. The extremist condition may be that ten points are allocated to one statement in a question. Please fill in the following form according to your actual situation.

I. The contribution I believe I can make to my team is that:

A. I can quickly recognize and find varieties of valuable resources and support from outside.
B. I can cooperate and work with people of all types.
C. I am born with a tendency to give creative suggestions.
D. I can find the most suitable people to carry out certain tasks and recommend them to other team members.
E. I can turn ideas, decisions or suggestions into feasible action plans.
F. I am willing to do things that others will not do.
G. I can remind other members of their performance gaps on a regular basis so that their behavior will not deviate from the expected track.

II. I may show the following shortcoming inside my team:

A. I will get worried if the tasks assigned to me by my team are ambiguous and unclear.
B. I prefer to have jobs done with the help of others rather than by myself.
C. I would rather search for support and resources from outside than ask for help from internal members.
D. I may be regarded by some team members as a nitpicker, which makes it hard for me to get on well with others.
E. I will not start any work until there is a feasible plan.
F. I may find it hard to stand out from the crowd as I overvalue my interpersonal relationship with others.
G. I am regarded as an idealist in the eyes of some team members.

III. When I carry out certain tasks together with other team members:

A. I am good at discovering the specialties and advantages of others.
B. I will always spend a lot of time formulating detailed plans before actions are taken.
C. I am experienced in proposing new ideas and solutions.
D. I am willing to accept the decisions agreed on by most team members even if they harm my own interests.
E. I am passionate about seeking resources that others in my team fail to discover in order to better accomplish the working objectives of the whole team.
F. I believe that my constructive criticism and warnings can help others make improvements.
G. I will never complain even if more tasks are assigned to me than to others

(continued)

TABLE 11.3 (Cont.)

Self-evaluation Table of Your Roles

Test Form of Team Roles

IV. One of my behavioral characteristics in the eyes of my team members is:

A. I am interested in knowing more about my colleagues.
B. I often challenge others' ideas in terms of feasibility and practicality.
C. I will criticize others for their wrongdoings in an open way.
D. I believe that I can turn the plans made by my superiors into expected results as long as they are correct.
E. I don't care if what I propose is considered strange or impracticable by others.
F. I am willing to build and improve relationships with people outside my team.
G. I can divide complicated tasks into several parts which are easier to be carried out by others

V. I am satisfied with my work because:

A. I have a strong crisis of conscience and can recognize potential risks earlier than others.
B. I am excited to be able to solve specific problems.
C. I feel that I am helpful to the promotion of interpersonal relationships between team members.
D. I have strong influence on the final action plans made by my team.
E. I can balance the interests between people outside the team and members inside the team.
F. I can make others willing to undertake the working tasks I assign to them.
G. I am glad that my talent of creativity is appreciated by others in my team.

VI. If a difficult and urgent job is assigned to me suddenly:

a. I will propose adjusting and improving the current action plans if there is no satisfying progress.
B. I will let others know all the possible risks, negative consequences and mistakes to be prevented.
C. I will consider the search for more resources and support as the first priority.
D. It will be hard for me to start my work without clear plans and instructions.
E. I always believe that good ideas will be more useful than working hard.
F. I will seek support and collaboration from team members as to things I am unable to do by myself.
G. I may put interpersonal relationships in front of my own interests when I have conflict with others.

TABLE 11.4

I.	F	D	E	C	A	G	B
IIO.	A	B	E	G	C	D	F
III.	G	A	B	C	E	F	D
IV.	D	G	B	E	F	C	A
V.	B	F	D	G	E	A	C
VI.	D	F	A	E	C	B	G
Total							
	Role of Blue	Role of Orange	Role of Green	Role of Cyan	Red of Purple	Role of Yellow	Role of Red

INFORMAL GROUP ALLIANCE

Informal groups will emerge naturally in large-scale teams. Members of these groups are bonded together due to common hobbies, similar backgrounds, complementary interests or close interpersonal relationships. Informal groups are formed by team members spontaneously in their daily interactions without legitimate recognition or approval from the organization. Generally speaking, there must be informal leaders of these groups who are respected and recognized by other members. Informal leaders win trust and recognition from other members by virtue of professional expertise, charm of personality, special background, mastery of resources or other advantages.

Once indirect leaders overlook the influence of informal groups on the cohesiveness of their teams, fractures and confrontation may emerge. If indirect leaders pay close attention to the existence of informal groups and make positive use of them, the cohesiveness of the whole team will be greatly improved. Therefore, informal groups can be regarded as double-edged swords that indirect leaders must attach much importance to. Such double-edged swords may hurt leaders and their teams if used inappropriately. They can also be quite helpful if mastered correctly. As the emergence of informal groups usually arises from the natural needs of team members' social interaction, leaders should neither restrain and even abolish them nor indulge and unconditionally cater to them. In sum, they shall deal with different types of informal groups in different ways.

Principles of Coping with Different Types of Informal Groups

Indirect leaders can categorize informal groups by two dimensions, which are degree of security and degree of compactness. Security here is opposite to destructiveness. If the informal group (abbreviated as IG) has positive, active and beneficial impact on the whole organization, it can be considered as IG with high degree of security. On the contrary, informal groups with low degree of security will have negative and harmful impact on the cohesiveness of teams. For example, some informal groups spread rumors, resist reforms, destroy internal trust, create conflicts and even cause talented employees to leave.

Compactness here is a definition in contrast to instability. Informal groups with a high degree of compactness tend to have stable members, acknowledged leaders, planned activities and frequent internal communication. Based on the dimension of security and the dimension of compactness, leaders can classify informal groups into four types as follows (see Figure 11.2):

1. Passive Informal Groups: Such informal groups have low degree of security as well as low degree of compactness. The relationship between members of passive informal groups is relatively weak and unstable. Without common goals, well-organized activities and

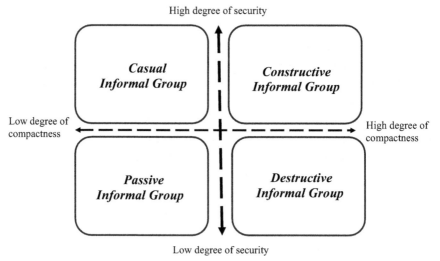

FIGURE 11.2
Four types of informal groups.

highly recognized leaders, the connection between members is very loose. Meanwhile, members of passive informal groups tend to be uncooperative and even hostile to commands from formal leaders of their organization.

2. Casual Informal Groups: Such informal groups have high degree of security and low degree of compactness. Members of casual informal groups are connected with each other due to similar habits, hobbies or interests. Such informal groups are not well organized and members tend to interact with each other casually. Therefore, such informal groups are not destructive and harmful to the cohesiveness of the whole team.

3. Destructive Informal Groups: Such informal groups have a high degree of compactness and low degree of security. Informal groups of this type are well organized and have sufficient abilities to fight against formal organizations for the benefits of their members. Meanwhile, members of such informal groups usually disobey the orders from formal organizations but obey the commands from informal leaders.

4. Constructive Informal Groups: Such informal groups have a high degree of security as well as a high degree of compactness. Informal groups of this type are supportive and helpful to their organization. Members of constructive informal groups are united closely by frequent interaction and smooth communication. For example, the Quality Control Group of Toyota was founded spontaneously by staff of the manufacturing department. Members will gather together after work for coffee and freely exchange their viewpoints on how to deal with manufacturing problems or product defects. In the end, they can always find out creative solutions through heated discussions.

As these four types of informal groups differ from each other greatly, it is better for leaders to refer to the following principles while coping with them (Table 11.5). Any type of informal group can turn into other types under certain circumstances. It is not impossible for passive or casual informal groups to transform into destructive formal groups.

For example, when a casual informal group conflicts with the formal organization, it is likely to become destructive if members choose to solve the conflict through confrontation and struggle. In another case, if a mighty leader emerges in a passive informal group, members will be united

TABLE 11.5

Principles of Coping with Four Types of Informal Groups

Types of Informal Groups	Corresponding Principles
Passive Informal Groups	• Indirect leaders need to identify influential members in passive informal groups and cultivate them into informal leaders. • Indirect leaders shall minimize the destructiveness of passive informal groups by building mutual trust and cooperative relationships with informal leaders.
Casual Informal Groups	• Indirect leaders shall offer support and resources to casual informal groups so as to better satisfy the needs of members. • Casual informal groups can be developed into constructive informal groups in a step-by-step way. They have the potential to be turned into an important driving force of cohesiveness enhancement inside leaders' organizations.
Destructive Informal Groups	• When destructive groups can't be managed and controlled in normal ways, indirect leaders need to punish or even remove the extremists of these groups resolutely so as to warn and intimidate other members.
Constructive Informal Groups	• Indirect leaders shall develop constructive informal groups into allies in their organizations by supplying more support and resources to them. • If possible, indirect leaders can further develop the leaders of constructive informal groups into formal managers at appropriate organizational levels.

around him or her and the group may become destructive. Therefore, leaders should not only pay attention to the transformation of existing informal groups, but also learn how to employ varieties of tactics to ally with informal groups, especially the destructive ones.

Five Critical Tactics of Informal Group Alliance

As informal groups are just like double-edged swords, leaders should not only make positive use of them but also guard against the destructive effect of these informal groups. Based on the experiences derived from numerous cases, there are five practical and feasible tactics that leaders can adopt to master these double-edged swords. The five tactics of informal group alliance include tactic of enticement, tactic of break up, tactic of penetration, tactic of lurk and tactic of creation, which are shown in Figure 11.3.

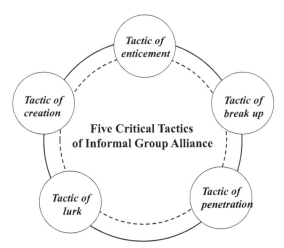

FIGURE 11.3
Five critical tactics of informal group alliance.

Tactic of Enticement

Indirect leaders can make full use of the influence and abilities of informal leaders by developing them into formal managers. Informal leaders who are willing to accept managerial positions offered by indirect leaders will be quite helpful to the promotion of organizational cohesiveness. The positions offered to informal leaders can be either official or semiofficial. Excellent leaders are good at creating various semiofficial positions tailor-made for the needs of informal leaders, such as head coach, chief controller, principal coordinator, senior consultant and project leader. Indirect leaders can recognize and accept the legitimate status of informal groups in various ways according to the different characteristics of these groups. For example, for informal groups composed of members with common hobbies in sports, indirect leaders can establish formal sport teams officially and subsidize these informal groups with funds and equipment.

Tactic of Breakup

Indirect leaders should think of ways to attract members of destructive informal groups to join in formal groups or other informal groups which are constructive. Indirect leaders can encourage members of informal groups to participate in various meetings, gatherings, outings or other activities held or recognized by the organization so as to clear up their misunderstanding toward others.

Tactic of Penetration

Leaders themselves can penetrate into informal groups by taking part in their activities and gatherings. By playing, eating, drinking and talking with members of these groups, leaders can eliminate the prejudices, hostile attitudes or even resistance from these members toward them. When indirect leaders successfully turn themselves into members of informal groups, they can exert their personal influence on other members so as to make positive use of these informal groups.

Tactic of Lurk

Indirect leaders can assign people they trust to join informal groups and take part in their activities. People who lurk in informal groups can keep leaders abreast of the dynamics and conditions of these groups. Leaders can take action in advance as soon as they are informed by their spies that some informal groups are developing into destructive ones. Indirect leaders can make positive use of the communication channels of informal groups. Information transmission in these informal communication channels is faster and more efficient. Therefore, indirect leaders can release information via these informal channels when they find formal communication channels are less effective.

Tactic of Creation

When formal organizations or positions fail to help leaders achieve expected management objectives, leaders can also choose to create some informal groups as their shadow teams. There are various forms of shadow teams, such as study groups, interest classes, culture salons, family gatherings and weekend tourism groups. Leaders can lower the degree of formal administration and allow self-government for these created informal groups, so that senses of ownership and belonging can be shared by all members. Regarding the lack of innovation and inadequacy of learning atmosphere in various departments, GE created an informal group called Work Out in the 1980s. This group was composed of employees working at various positions including managers, secretaries, engineers, workers of production lines and even clients or suppliers. They usually gathered in a room to discuss problems and opportunities in certain areas. Such an informal group tended to respond quickly and decisively to the best advice produced, regardless of who raised them. The group, work out, is now one of the important symbols of GE culture.

In this case, when formal organizations and mechanisms were no more helpful to the promotion of innovation, GE created an informal group called work out. According to the five critical tactics of informal group alliance, GE adopted the tactic of creation. Many other well-known enterprises and excellent indirect leaders are also good at creating informal groups to accomplish their leadership and management goals.

Many top-level managers are willing to spend time playing ball games, dining or even singing and dancing with employees no matter how tight their schedules are. They expect to build mutual trust with important informal groups and win support from their members by doing so. According to the five critical tactics of informal group alliance, the tactic of penetration is adopted by these leaders.

Some other leaders are good at releasing news and transmitting information through informal channels so as to achieve communication objectives unattainable through formal communication channels. They are obviously using the tactic of lurk. While for those informal groups with mighty leaders, excellent indirect leaders will choose to adopt the tactic of enticement or tactic of breakup.

TRUST CIRCLE

Trust building is critical to the enhancement of the overall cohesive force of the leader's teams. Indirect leaders should understand that large-scale teams are usually composed of various small groups as well as several hidden informal groups. If indirect leaders fail to build, expand and spread trust inside the whole team, then the cohesiveness among team members will be greatly weakened due to inadequate trust foundation.

Therefore, indirect leaders must be devoted to building a high degree of trust in their teams. Trust Circle Building is a useful and proved way of enhancing cohesiveness between team members that leaders can learn from and put into practice. The trust circle usually originates from the credible interpersonal relationship between leaders and several core members of the team. Then these core team members radiate the trust outside of the circle to other members of the whole team.

In other words, due to the help from core trust circle members, leaders are able to build trust with people outside the circle indirectly and transmit the relationship of trust to every member of the whole organization. Actually, members of the trust circle will form their own sub trust circle composed of people around them. The formal communication channels of most organizations and teams can transmit fundamental information, such as policies, regulations, rules and requirements from the top down, but many of them fail to convey trust between team members. The trust circle is a special communication channel built by leaders themselves to transmit and radiate trust in an informal way.

Four Critical Steps of Trust Circle Building

Trust circles are groups formed by and around indirect leaders through various ways of communication, interaction and organization. Indirect leaders expand the scale of a trust circle gradually and encourage trust circle members to build their own sub trust circle connecting people around them. There are four critical steps of a trust circle building that leaders should attach great importance to, which are effective establishment of the trust circle, steady expansion of the trust circle, outward radiation of the trust circle and regular evaluation of the trust circle.

Establishment of Trust Circle

It is not necessary for leaders to pursue the rapid expansion of the trust circle in the beginning. The quality of initial trust circle is critical to its future development. It is important for indirect leaders to choose the right candidates of trust circles' initial members and the following criteria are worthy of leader's reference.

1. Proximity in space: It is better for indirect leaders to choose those who live and work in close connection with each other as initial members because they have enough time to participate in various activities and events of the trust circle.

2. High frequency of interaction: It is meaningful for indirect leaders to choose those who have frequent interactions with each other as the initial members of the trust circle.
3. Consistency in value: Indirect leaders must invite staff with similar values and the same attitudes to join the trust circle as initial members. Consistency in value and ideology is the premise of trust building in the circle.
4. Complementary needs: Each member of the trust circle has his or her own needs in various areas. Leaders should choose those whose needs are complementary to each other as initial members. If members can satisfy his or her personal needs with the help and support from other members, then the trust circles will be more stable and attractive.

Expansion of Trust Circle

After establishing the initial trust circles which are usually small in scale, indirect leaders need to expand their trust circles in a step-by-step way. Initial members are requested to recommend candidates and strict evaluation will be made by all initial members before any new member is adopted.

Radiation of Trust Circle

Each member of a trust circle is responsible for the radiation of trust to others around him or her. Trust circle members are responsible for transmitting what they have learned, experienced and inspired inside the trust circle to people surrounding them.

Evaluation of Trust Circle

Indirect leaders shall regularly evaluate the level of trust between members in their trust circles. What's more, leaders should also assess members' performance on trust transmission toward people outside the circle. Indirect leaders shall pay special attention to the control of speed and scale in the process of trust circle building. They shall not be too ambitious in the beginning period and quality should be placed ahead of quantity. Trust circles are not only circles made up of individuals, they are essentially circles made up of individuals with mutual trust. If indirect leaders fail to control the speed of a trust circle's expansion, internal trust will probably decrease dramatically, triggered by the rapid growth of the number of new members. Increasing misunderstanding, distrust and conflicts may emerge and lead to the collapse of whole trust circle.

Six Bonds of Building a Trust Circle

The success of trust circle building depends largely on whether there are enough trust bonds binding members together within the circle developed by leaders. In any highly successful trust circle, there must be several trust bonds linking its members in addition to the monetary bond. These trust bonds are just like the common blood shared by all the members of the circle. A perfect trust circle usually achieves high levels of mutual trust between its members through the establishment of six trust bonds, which are bond of common background, bond of common hobby, bond of common interest, bond of common working, bond of mutual understanding and bond of common value (see Figure 11.4).

Bond of Common Background

Common background of most members is the first bond of a perfect trust circle. Leaders shall find as many people with common background or common origin as possible to build the initial trust circle. The so-called common origin may include the relationship of relatives, schoolfellows,

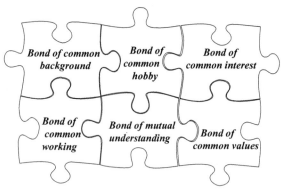

FIGURE 11.4
Six bonds of a trust circle.

fellow-townsman, and so on. On the other hand, leaders need to create more common experiences between members of the same trust circle. Unforgettable and memorable common experiences will leave indelible imprints in the hearts of members and bind them tightly. For example, many senior generals of the armed forces will choose subordinates who have fought shoulder to shoulder in great battles with them as members of their trust circles, since the heartfelt common experience of that battle will be transformed into trust bonds tying core members together.

Bond of Common Hobby

The second bond of a perfect trust circle is the common habits and hobbies shared by most members. Similarity in habits and hobbies will greatly increase the frequency of interactions between members and make the trust circle more active and stable. Indirect leaders need to find out habits/hobbies that are popular among members and promote them to be the common habits/hobbies of the trust circle. Some leaders also choose to develop their own habits/hobbies into the common ones shared by all the members. Excellent leaders always encourage and promote habits/hobbies which are beneficial to the development and growth of members, such as reading, traveling, physical exercise and voluntary work.

Bond of Common Interest

Leaders shall motivate and encourage trust circle members to support each other at work as well as in life. Members of the same trust circle have different advantages, resources, abilities and social connections, so they are complementary to each other in the pursuit of personal interests. If members can solve problems for each other, share resources with each other and bring benefits to each other, the whole trust circle will be stabilized and reinforced by common interests. Leaders can enhance the willingness of trust circle members to sacrifice for the benefits of others by setting good examples with their own words and behavior.

Bond of Common Working

Leaders should involve members of trust circles in programs or assignments that need high levels of cooperation and coordination. Members of the trust circle will build mutual trust and eliminate estrangement rapidly when they are performing and accomplishing tasks together. Indirect leaders can elaborately create some challenges or trouble for members of the trust circle to deal with and overcome together. Only under external pressures will members of the trust circle be highly united and closely bound. Indirect leaders shall also participate in these challenging tasks and work together with other members.

Bond of Mutual Understanding

Leaders can enhance mutual understanding between trust circle members through continuous emotional exchange and in-depth communication. Brainstorming, communions, tea or coffee parties and heart-to-heart talks shall be held frequently so that members can freely speak about their own state of mind. Leaders shall listen to the feelings, complaints and expectations of core members of the trust circle one by one on a regular basis. What's more, leaders' own state of mind must also be known to, and understood by, trust circle members.

Bond of Common Values

It is necessary for indirect leaders to define core values of the trust circle and make them accepted by all the members through various ways of promotion and publicity. Core values shared by trust circle members as one of the most important trust bonds should be built with continuous effort. Members are also requested by leaders to act as the propagandists and promotors of core values of their trust circles. With their efforts, core values advocated by indirect leaders can radiate outside the trust circle to more and more people.

Part IV

Organizational Executive Leadership

12

Three Dynamic Optimizations of Organizational Executive Leadership

Ray was the CEO of a hi-tech company that was in a stage of stable development. Ray was a man of his word and managed his company with rigorous regulations and strict disciplines. Many veteran employees were dedicated to assist and follow him because they recognized his ability and character. Ray gradually reduced his involvement in the daily management of his company, hoping to have his son, Raymond, take over from him as the CEO.

In order to further increase market share, Ray's company merged and acquired its biggest competitor. Ray thought the management challenges resulting from this acquisition would offer precious learning opportunities to Raymond. Raymond joined his father's company two years ago after his graduation from a well-known university. He was appointed as the vice president of the company soon although there were objections from core members of Ray's management team. The merger of the two companies did result in a substantial increase in terms of market share, while the negative impact of this acquisition far exceeded Ray's anticipation. Due to the vast differences between these two companies in terms of corporate culture, values and behavioral modes, there was little mutual trust between members of the new management team. Managers from Ray's company looked down upon their peers from the rival company, leading to lots of communication barriers and frequent conflicts.

However, Ray and Raymond firmly believed that this was a normal phenomenon resulting from merger and acquisition. Therefore, they were unwilling to change their existing ways of management as well as their leadership styles. They thought that the management pattern which had been proved effective for over 10 years should be kept unchanged. But the situation became much worse than Ray had expected. Interest groups began to emerge and conflicts between the original staff of the two companies were so fierce that no efforts of mediation helped. Morale of the management team decreased dramatically and staff in key positions began to leave.

Although Raymond realized the severity of the situation later, he still hesitated in making drastic changes for fear of possible negative effects. Ray was kept in the dark until there were open disputes and quarrels during the management meeting he chaired. Then Ray was ill in the hospital due to excessive tiredness and anxiety. Raymond, who took charge of the daily affairs of the company, was just like an ant on a hot pan. He was kept busy putting out fires everywhere. But it was almost impossible for him to handle so many tough challenges, as he was lacking adequate front-line management experience.

Many unsolved problems were kicked back to Ray who was lying in the hospital. It was not until then that Ray realized that his son, who used to be energetic and vigorous, was of no use at such a critical moment. Ray had to come back from his illness and cope with all the challenges by himself. What he needed to decide first was whether Raymond should be dismissed from his position. Ray consulted with all the members of his core management team one by one and drew conclusions based on his summary of different opinions.

But Ray's way of decision-making was opposed by most managers who used to work for the rival company. They did not think Ray's decision-making mode was transparent enough and insisted that a meeting attended by all levels of managers should be held. What's more, they declared that this decision should be made in a more democratic way through voting by ballot. Faced with such a fresh new mode of decision-making, Ray was really at a loss. As the boss as well as CEO, Ray was not only the face-to-face leader of his direct subordinates and the indirect leader of all the employees under his management, but also the organizational executive leader of his company.

Over the past decade, Ray's exemplary behaviors and good personal character have helped him win continuous trust, recognition and support from his direct subordinates, which proved that he performed well in terms of followership. Over the past decade, Ray had developed many talented subordinates who were both competent and loyal, which manifested that he was also an outstanding face-to-face leader. And over the past decade, he had successfully built and promoted the centripetal force, executive force and cohesive force of his team, indicating that he was also a qualified indirect leader. However, at the critical stage of acquisition and his son's succession, Ray failed to prove himself as a qualified organizational executive leader. As the fourth shifting-gear of leadership, organizational executive leadership exhibits leaders' abilities to adapt to organizational changes through dynamic adjustments and optimization of their leadership modes.

THREE DYNAMIC OPTIMIZATIONS OF ORGANIZATIONAL EXECUTIVE LEADERSHIP

There could be abundant topics or content that organizational executive leadership may include, among which these three dynamic optimizations should be put in first priority by leaders: *Dynamic optimization of talent pool, dynamic optimization decision-making mode* and *dynamic optimization of leadership.*

Dynamic Optimization of Talent Pool

To better achieve the strategic goals and plans of their organizations, organizational executive leaders should attach much importance to the development of more excellent leaders at all levels of their organizations. They should build in advance leadership talent pools in order to reserve, develop and deploy talented future leaders.

Dynamic Optimization of Decision-making Mode

Organizational executive leaders have to make decisions on a variety of major issues regularly. Compared with mid-level and grassroots leaders, the validity of the decisions made by organizational executive leaders tends to have a huge impact on the future development of the whole organization. Organizational executive leaders must adopt different decision-making modes under different circumstances. Differences in decision-making ways will greatly affect employees' willingness of implementation.

FIGURE 12.1
Three dynamic optimizations.

Dynamic Optimization of Leadership Style

Organizational executive leaders must understand that the whole organization is in a constant state of change instead of remaining unchanged. They need to adjust their own leadership styles once the development stage of their organization changes. In other words, organizational executive leaders should learn to adopt different leadership styles at different stages of organizational development (Figure 12.1).

In the case of Ray, he failed to cultivate qualified successors in advance for his forthcoming retirement. On the contrary, the decision of his son's succession at the critical period of merger and acquisition was hasty and risky. As an organizational executive leader, Ray was not qualified in terms of dynamic optimization of talent pool. When Ray had to make decisions on whether his son should stay or leave, he still adopted his original way of decision-making by consulting with core subordinates one by one. He failed to adjust and optimize his decision-making mode under the new circumstances. Moreover, Ray also failed to realize that the development stage of his company had changed greatly after the merger and acquisition. Therefore, his leadership style should have also been adjusted to better match the new stage of organizational development.

DYNAMIC OPTIMIZATION OF ORGANIZATIONAL TALENT POOL

Organizational executive leaders should shift their focus from developing themselves into excellent leaders to cultivating more excellent leaders at all levels of their organizations. They need to analyze the bench strength of their management team and build stabilized pipelines of leadership development. Dynamic optimization of the leadership talent pool would be beneficial to the stability and sustainable development of any type of organizations.

Therefore, a core responsibility of any organizational executive leader is to build leadership development pipelines for his or her organization in order to develop and retain talented leaders at various organizational levels. Some high-level leaders still rely heavily on their personal abilities or even personality cult while leading their organizations. As a result, once these leaders can't continue their work due to health problems or other reasons, the whole organization may encounter turbulence or even collapse.

An Wang, an extraordinary inventor, entrepreneur and scientist, founded a computer company named Wang Laboratories which was once well-known worldwide. He used to be ranked as the fifth wealthiest person in America and was recognized as a miracle in the world of Chinese people. However, the successor chosen by him turned out to be the gravedigger of his business empire and Wang Laboratories was put into bankruptcy in less than six years.

The Significance of Building Leadership Development Pipelines

Leaders should pay close attention to five major phenomena of inadequate succession planning or poor talent-pool building, which are listed specifically in Table 12.1.

Leadership pipeline development refers to the process in which top leaders of the organization consistently identify, track and develop high-potential talent of key positions. High-potential talents are those who are believed

TABLE 12.1

Five Major Phenomena of Inadequate Succession Planning

Lack of Succession Planning	Many high-level leaders do not have enthusiasm as well as foresight in reserving and developing successors for existing managers at various organizational levels. They don't have a sense of crisis and consider talent-pool building unnecessary and unworthy of doing.
Lack of Systematic Cultivation	Many candidates are chosen and appointed in an unscheduled way. They don't have qualified abilities and qualities and are not competent enough for their management positions when assuming responsibility.
Lack of Smooth Handover	In some organizations, there are always disagreements and even conflicts between existing leaders and their successors due to the lack of adequate co-work and mutual trust.
Lack of Preplanned Alternatives	Some high-level leaders may quit, leave or become unable to continue their work due to various reasons, which may result in a huge crisis to the whole organization if qualified successors can't take their place in a short time.
Lack of Talent Flow	If there is no mechanism of talent flow in the organization, prospective leaders will have limited chances of future promotion. They will probably choose to leave and the bench strength of key managerial positions will be weakened.

by their superiors to be qualified for managerial positions at higher levels. The significance of building leadership development pipelines lies in three areas:

- Organizational executive leaders can reserve and develop abundant future leaders through the establishment and development of leadership talent pools. High-potential talents are identified, assessed and cultivated in a systematic and continuous way and the bench strength of key positions will be greatly enhanced.
- Middle-level and grassroots managers will be offered more opportunities to exhibit their talent and potential of leadership in front of their superiors.
- Excellent talents can have more chances of getting promoted so that their loyalty and devotion to their organizations will increase greatly.

The managerial positions involved in leadership pipeline development and succession planning include not only top and high-level executives but also mid-level and grassroots supervisors. The sustainable cultivation and development of future leaders at various levels are significant to the continuity of organizational policies and cultures.

Four Strategies of Developing Leadership Pipelines

Henry Chow set about introducing an internationally recognized leadership development system in China after taking the position as chairman of the board of IBM Great China. Managers of his company were told that development of direct subordinates would be included as an important part of their core responsibilities. Managers at all levels in his organization were asked to select and determine their successors right after they took office. Future leaders were informed that they had been identified and valued by the company and there would be professional guidance and abundant activities enabling them to be qualified for higher positions. What Henry Chow brought to his company was widely recognized as a bench plan in IBM.

IBM's bench plan is a successful example showing the significance of building a leadership development pipeline. Then, what specific strategies could organizational executive leaders adopt to make the development of a leadership pipeline more effective in real practice? There are in total four strategies worthy of leaders' reference which are described in detail as follows.

Incorporate Successor Development in the Performance Evaluation of Existing Leaders

Existing leaders may lack enough willingness and motivation to develop potential leaders and successors due to various reasons. Successor development should be included as an indispensable component of the performance evaluation of existing leaders. Organizational executive leaders need to evaluate whether existing leaders have the willingness to reserve and develop high-potential employees, since the conservative attitudes of many existing leaders are one of the causes of the failure of succession plans. If existing leaders do not take the initiative in cultivating prospective successors, then the shaping of leadership development pipelines will encounter a lot of obstacles.

Therefore, organizational executive leaders have to fully communicate with managers at all levels and obtain their understanding in, as well as support for, succession planning. In addition, discovery and cultivation of prospective leaders should be included in the overall evaluation and incentive system of existing managers. Organizational executive leaders must formulate and publicize rewarding measures for those who succeed in selecting and cultivating future leaders of their organizations. IBM's bench plan was featured by the mandatory requirements of successor development for existing leaders.

Link Succession Planning with Existing HR Management System

Leadership pipeline development and succession planning should be linked with the existing HR management system. Heads of HR departments should be asked to shoulder direct responsibilities of developing future leaders and building leadership talent pools. IBM's success in the cultivation of successors was closely linked to the participation and contribution of its HR team. The development of future leaders should be the core function of HR management and core responsibility of senior HR personnel. Leadership pipeline development cannot succeed without the assistance from and involvement of the organization's HR system. Recruitment and selection, training and development, performance appraisal, compensation positioning and other operational functions of HR management should be examined and improved to better support the construction of leadership pipelines.

Identify the Gap of Job Requirements Between the Current Position and the Future Position of Successors

Competency models of successors' future positions should be built and specified. Analysis of the gap of job requirements between the current position and the future position will be helpful to the formulation of talent development plans. Organizational executive leaders should find out the differences between the KSA (knowledge, skill and ability) of current positions and that of the future positions of successors. By comparing the KSA of current positions with that of the future positions, organizational executive leaders can plan and implement strategies of future leader development based on the identification of the competency gap of successors.

Plans of future leader development in many organizations failed because they were merely based on the job requirements of current positions.

Establish Diversified Selection and Cultivation Mechanisms for Prospective Leaders

Based on the results of periodical performance evaluation, potential leaders will be categorized into different types so as to develop them with differentiated channels and strategies. The process of leadership pipeline development normally starts from the performance evaluation of existing talents. Differentiated training and cultivation programs will be planned and conducted for talents with different performance evaluation results. The talents of potential leaders will be classified into four quadrants, which are presented in the following illustration (Figure 12.2).

Quadrant I : High Performance/Low Potential

For employees in this quadrant, continuous assessment as well as development should be done mainly by the HR department on a regular basis. It is suggested that career development of such employees should be shifted from the managerial path to the professional path if they fail to make expected improvement in terms of leadership within a certain period of time. Leaders should formulate either a managerial career path or professional career path for different talents.

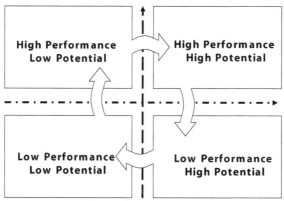

FIGURE 12.2
Four types of potential leaders.

Quadrant II : High Performance/High Potential

Employees in this quadrant are the main sources of leadership talents in succession plans, who can be promoted in three different ways:

- Ready to go: They can be promoted to take on higher positions at once.
- Ready to go later: They can be promoted right after a short period of special training or coaching.
- Ready to go later if qualified: They should not be promoted until they are proved to be competent and qualified enough after further training, appraisal or job rotation.

Quadrant III : Low Performance/High Potential

HR department should do in-depth performance analyses and diagnoses for employees in quadrant III, finding out the root causes of their poor performance so as to formulate improvement plans. Employees in this quadrant should be offered sufficient tailor-made professional training and coaching. If they fail to make improvement after systematic training, root causes of low performance should be further analyzed and found out. If problems lie in the mismatch between people and position, then job rotations should be recommended and implemented.

Quadrant IV: Low Performance/Low Potential

Employees in this quadrant should be included in the PEI (Performance Examination and Improvement) programs so as to exploit their potential for further development with combinations of methods and resources. Those who prove to be unqualified and incompetent should be laid off.

DYNAMIC OPTIMIZATION OF DECISION-MAKING MODES

Organizational executive leaders are on top of their organizational pyramids. Therefore, decisions made by them are closely related to the fate of the whole organization and their decision-making abilities are indispensable parts of their overall leadership. What's more, organizational executive leaders should adopt differentiated decision-making modes under different circumstances.

Four Modes of Decision-making

There are four modes of decision-making for organizational executive leaders to choose from in different situations. Autocratic way of decision-making, advisory way of decision-making, consultative way of decision-making and democratic way of decision-making can all be highly effective if employed in appropriate situations (Table 12.2).

Autocratic Way of Decision-making

Leaders make decisions on certain important matters fully based on their own judgments, experience and knowledge without discussing or asking the relevant subordinates. Leaders who don't have confidence in the decision-making abilities of their subordinates or who don't attach much importance to the participation of subordinates in decision-making will prefer to adopt such a way of decision-making. As employees are not allowed to be involved in the process of decision-making, their understanding in and recognition of the decisions made by their leaders will be lowered.

TABLE 12.2

Four Modes of Decision-making

Autocratic way of decision-making	Leaders make decisions by themselves without communicating and consulting with others in their organizations.
Advisory way of decision-making	Leaders communicate and consult with subordinates separately and make decisions on their own based on summaries of personal opinions of different subordinates.
Consultative way of decision-making	Leaders call together all their subordinates and encourage them to raise their opinions and advice in an open way. Disagreements and debates between subordinates are allowed. The final judgments and decisions will be made by leaders on their own.
Democratic way of decision-making	Leaders call together all the subordinates and leave the final decisions to them. Group decision-making ways such as vote by ballot will be adopted if consensus are difficult to reach.

Most leaders who are accustomed to an autocratic way of decision-making tend to be assertive and not open-minded. If leaders are lacking enough information and resources at hand, the autocratic way of decision-making will be risky and probably destructive. But sometimes, leaders are forced to adopt such a way of decision-making due to the limitation of time.

Advisory Way of Decision-making

Leaders communicate and consult with each of their subordinates individually about the decisions to be made. The purpose and challenges of decision-making are made known to leaders' subordinates. Based on the collected opinions from different subordinates, leaders make final decisions on their own.

An advisory way of decision-making can promote the sense of participation and involvement on the part of subordinates. In addition, arguments and conflicts between subordinates with different opinions will be avoided because leaders communicate and discuss with different subordinates one by one. The advisory way of decision-making is more time-consuming compared to the autocratic way; however, if better decisions can be made and the understanding and recognition from subordinates can be enhanced, an advisory way of decision-making is worthy of adoption.

Consultative Way of Decision-making

Leaders adopting the consultative way of decision-making will always call together relevant subordinates to discuss the decisions to be made openly in a meeting. Leaders explain to all the subordinates involved the purpose of decision-making and encourage them to raise opinions as well as advice. In the process of discussion, leaders play the role of encouragers who motivate and inspire participants to propose various viewpoints and alternatives in an open way. In the end, leaders will make their final decisions by integrating the opinions of subordinates with their own experiences. What's more, leaders should also illustrate the rationality of final decisions to subordinates who have disagreements.

The consultative way of decision-making may be much more time-consuming and inefficient in terms of speediness. However, employees' full involvement and participation in such decision-making will greatly improve their understanding and acceptance of the final decisions. A consultative way of decision-making will promote both the validity of final decisions and the willingness of subordinates to implement these decisions. However, if there are great divergences and disagreements between subordinates, a consultative way of decision-making may lead to severe conflicts between participants in the process of open discussion.

Democratic Way of Decision-making

The democratic way of decision-making features full involvement and participation of subordinates. Leaders will leave the rights of making decisions to subordinates and fully support the final decisions made by the whole team. The democratic way of decision-making is the most time-consuming and complicated mode among the four. But it is probably the most acceptable one to staff who exhibit strong desires to participate in decision-making.

There are also risks of wrong decisions made in such a democratic way if employees choose to vote on the stance of their own interests instead of the interests of the whole organization. In particular, when the decisions are closely linked to the vital benefits of employees involved, the orientation of decision-making may deviate from the expected track. A democratic way of decision-making is the most open and interactive one among the four. But it is also an extreme way of decision-making, just like the autocratic mode. Some leaders may leave the whole decision-making process to subordinates and assume no responsibilities for any wrong decisions in the name of democracy (see Figure 12.3).

Seven Questions to be Reflected Upon While Choosing Decision-making Modes

Leaders should understand that each decision-making mode has its own advantages and disadvantages. If leaders pursue sufficiency of information and full participation of employees, the efficiency and speediness of decision-making will be sacrificed. On the other hand, the pursuit of rapidity and time saving in decision-making may come at the cost of information adequacy and employee participation. Indeed, the effectiveness of each mode depends on the characteristics of the decisions to be made and the circumstances decision makers are faced with. Organizational

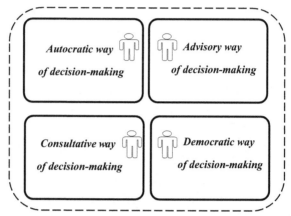

FIGURE 12.3
Four decision-making modes.

TABLE 12.3

Seven Questions to be Reflected upon While Choosing Decision-making Modes

Seven Questions	Description of Seven Questions
Question A	Is it urgent for me to have the decision made?
Question B	Do I have enough information and resources to make a correct decision?
Question C	Will the decision to be made have long-term or widespread impact on my organization?
Question D	Will there be severe consequences if I make a wrong decision?
Question E	Is my subordinates' participation in decision-making important to their recognition of and implementation of the decision?
Question F	Are there serious disagreements among my subordinates about the decision to be made?
Question G	Is there enough willingness from my subordinates to participate in decision-making?

executive leaders need to fully consider the following seven issues while choosing from these decision-making modes (see Table 12.3).

Vincent was the production director of a large manufacturing enterprise that introduced a new working system recently. To his surprise, expected improvement of productivity and promotion of efficiency did not come into reality. On the contrary, the efficiency of manufacturing started to decline and the production yield decreased gradually. Vincent firmly believed that these problems had nothing to do with the machines of the new system as there were many other companies that succeeded in upgrading productivity by using the same types of machine. Vincent was told by technicians of the supplier that everything was fine with these machines based on their careful check. Vincent felt the problem might be caused by the mismatch between hardware and software in the new system. But not all of his direct subordinates had similar viewpoints. There were in total four mid-level managers who directly reported to Vincent and their opinions on the decline of productivity differed from each other. Some believed that it was caused by insufficient operating skills of workers, some insisted that it was due to the lack of standardized operating procedures and others thought that it was rooted in the disappointing rewarding mechanism. Obviously, each of Vincent's direct subordinates had his own views on such a problem.

One morning Vincent received a phone call from Bill, his boss and CEO of the company. Bill said that he had been informed of the situation and he would never interfere in Vincent's decision-making. He also promised that he would agree on and support any decision made by Vincent. Bill suggested that Vincent didn't have to rush into decisions and it was better for him to maintain the current situation for a period of time. Vincent and his mid-level managers were worried about the continuous decline in productivity and they knew that the grassroots subordinates were also waiting for their decisions. Which one of the four decision-making modes was most suitable for him to adopt?

This is a typical case about the choice of decision-making modes for organizational executive leaders. Vincent's decision-making situation analyzed by the seven questions is listed as follows:

1. Question A: Is it urgent for me to have the decision made?
   With the support from his CEO, Vincent had no time pressure and didn't have to make an urgent or hasty decision.
2. Question B: Do I have enough information and resources to make the right decision?
   In this case, Vincent didn't have the abundant information and resources necessary for making a high-quality decision.
3. Question C: Will the decision to be made have long-term or wide-spread impact on my organization?
   Actually, the decision to be made by Vincent had a significant as well as long-term impact on his company.

4. Question D: Will there be severe consequences if I make a wrong decision?

   There were huge risks after Vincent made a wrong decision.

5. Question E: Is my subordinates' participation in decision-making important to their recognition of and implementation of the decision?

   Subordinates' participation in decision-making was critical to their acceptance of the final decision made by Vincent.

6. Question F: Are there serious disagreements among my subordinates about the decision to be made?

   There were severe divergences and conflicts between Vincent's direct subordinates in the process of decision-making.

7. Question G: Is there enough willingness from my subordinates to participate in decision-making?

   In this case, Vincent's subordinates showed great willingness to participate in the decision-making process.

In-depth consideration of these seven questions can help leaders choose and adopt the most correct way of decision-making. Vincent did not have any time pressure so he was able to spend more time on the decision-making process. He did not have plenty of information needed for a high-quality decision which would have a long-term impact on his company. Meanwhile, employees' participation in decision-making was indispensable and severe consequences would be caused by wrong decisions. Therefore, in this case, the autocratic way of decision-making was not suitable.

As there was disagreement between Vincent's subordinates, the adoption of a democratic way of decision-making might lead to severe conflicts and consensus couldn't be reached within a short period of time. Therefore, the democratic way of decision-making did not fit with Vincent's situation in this case. Which of the remaining two is better, advisory mode or consultative mode? As far as this case was concerned, Vincent could begin with the advisory mode so as to find out whether the divergence between different subordinates was too large to be eliminated. If the divergence was found to be not very serious, he could then call together all the subordinates for a meeting to openly discuss the decision and transform from advisory mode into consultative mode. But if consensus was impossible to reach and conflicts between subordinates deteriorated during the open discussion, he should abandon the consultative way of decision-making and restart the advisory mode.

DYNAMIC OPTIMIZATION OF LEADERSHIP STYLES

The development of any organization is to change dynamically. Organizational executive leaders should keenly recognize the change of the development stage of their organizations so as to adjust their leadership styles accordingly.

Four Stages of Organizational Development

How can leaders accurately recognize the development stage of their organizations? There are two indicators based on which leaders are able to define their organizations' development stages, which are *level of organizational maturity* and *level of organizational conformity*.

Level of Organizational Maturity

Highly mature organizations have rich experiences and plenty of resources in daily operations and are able to accomplish missions and objectives without leaders' intervention or involvement. In contrast, organizations with a low level of maturity are not competent or capable enough to achieve expected objectives independently. Leaders should be very involved in the daily operation of these organizations.

Level of Organizational Conformity

Members of organizations with a high level of conformity always show a high degree of recognition and acceptance of orders, commands and assignments from leaders and are quite willing to implement whatever is requested to do from the top. On the contrary, members in organizations with a low level of conformity often refuse to accept commands from their leaders and are likely to do what is prohibited by leaders. Development stages of any organization can be summarized and categorized into four based on these two indicators, which include stage of mc, stage of mC, stage of MC and stage of Mc.

Development Stage of mc: Low Level of Maturity and Low Level of Conformity

Organizations in such a development stage are not competent or capable enough to accomplish missions and achieve goals independently without deep involvement of leaders. What's more, members always show a low level of recognition and acceptance of orders, requirements, commands and assignments from leaders.

Development Stage of mC: Low Level of Maturity but High Level of Conformity

Organizations in such a development stage are not competent or capable enough to accomplish missions and achieve goals independently without deep involvement of leaders. However, willingness and enthusiasm of organizational members in obeying orders from leaders and executing missions assigned by leaders are quite high.

Development Stage of MC: High Level of Maturity and High Level of Conformity

Organizations in such a development stage have plenty of experience and resources in daily operation and can achieve expected performance objectives without leaders' involvement. What's more, most organizational members show a high degree of recognition and acceptance of orders, requests, commands and assignments from leaders.

Development Stage of Mc: High Level of Maturity but Low Level of Conformity

Organizations in such a development stage have rich experience and resources in daily operation and are able to achieve expected performance objectives without leaders' involvement. But members in such organizations often refuse to accept commands from their leaders and are likely to do what is prohibited by leaders.

Leadership Style Composed of Three Leadership Behaviors

Leaders differ from each other in terms of leadership styles. Some leaders are very amiable and good at building interpersonal rapport and emotional bonds with team members, while some are quite mighty in terms of their leadership styles and love to manage mainly by directing, monitoring, criticizing and even punishing others. Some other leaders are supportive and always willing to offer various guidance, assistance, help and backup to team members.

People with different leadership styles can all be extraordinary leaders. It is also important for leaders to know clearly the determinants of leadership styles so that they can flexibly adapt to the development stage of their organizations. Actually, leadership style is determined by three different types of leadership behaviors which include *interpersonal behaviors, supportive behaviors,* and *controlling behaviors.*

Interpersonal Behaviors

Interpersonal behaviors refer to a leader's behaviors of maintaining good interpersonal relationships and building emotional bonds with other organizational members. Interpersonal behaviors help leaders narrow psychological distance with team members, win trust from subordinates and eliminate misunderstanding of others. What's more, interpersonal behaviors are usually featured by the establishment of close private relationships between leaders and other organizational members.

Supportive Behaviors

Supportive behaviors include various forms of help and support offered by leaders to organizational members for their successful accomplishment of performance objectives. Supportive behaviors can include varieties of training and coaching supplied to employees as well as onsite co-work and backup by leaders. It is also considered as supportive behavior of leaders to help employees win more resources, benefits and policy support from the top. Supportive behaviors of leaders are aimed at improving the abilities of organizational members to better accomplish missions and attain goals.

Controlling Behaviors

Controlling behaviors refer to leaders' deep intervention in employees' daily behavior as well as implementation processes so as to rectify deviations and guard against risks. Leaders who use controlling behaviors frequently tend to be mighty and tough in personality. They attach greater importance to the achievement of results than to their interpersonal relationships with employees.

Different leadership styles are originated from the combination of these three leadership behaviors in different proportions. There is no good or bad leadership style. The effectiveness of leadership styles is determined by the extent to which leadership styles match the development stage of leaders' organizations.

Leadership Styles and Corresponding Organizational Development Stages

Leaders should switch their leadership styles once the development stage of their organizations change. In other words, leadership styles need to be in accordance with the development stage of leaders' organizations.

Leadership Style of Partnering for the Development Stage of mc

At the stage of mc, the mutual understanding and trust between leaders and employees are in urgent need of improvement. Leaders need to use more interpersonal behaviors so as to build harmonious relationships with organizational members and eliminate their misunderstanding as well as collisions with leaders. At this organizational development stage, an organization's capability of accomplishing given goals is inadequate and the willingness of organizational members to obey leaders' instructions and orders is also low. Leaders must enhance supportive behaviors, trying best to provide various support and help to organizational members for their successful accomplishment of given goals. The supportive behavior of leaders is aimed at increasing organizational maturity.

In addition, there must emerge varieties of mistakes, errors, emergencies or risks from an employee's implementation of missions at the stage of mc which is featured by low level of maturity and low level of conformity. Therefore, leaders should also employ more controlling behaviors. In conclusion, leaders should choose to show the leadership style of partnering, which is featured by more interpersonal behaviors, more supportive behaviors and more controlling behaviors at the organizational development stage of mc.

Leadership Style of Coaching for the Development Stage of mC

At the stage of mC, organizational members recognize, accept, follow and obey the instructions and commands from leaders. It is not necessary for leaders to employ lots of interpersonal behaviors since the relationships between members and leaders are already good enough. What's more, excessive interpersonal behaviors of leaders may lead to employees' confusion about the difference between working relationships and private relationships.

At this development stage, the overall ability to accomplish goals and complete missions of the organization is inadequate and the competences of most organizational members need to be improved. Leaders should use more supportive behaviors to promote the level of maturity of the whole organization. Furthermore, leaders should also enhance their controlling behavior at the development stage of mC. Employees in immature organizations will be likely to encounter problems and make mistakes in the process of execution due to their lack of necessary experience, abilities and resources. Additionally, there will be little resistance to the controlling behavior of leaders from employees because of the high level of organizational conformity.

In summary, leaders should choose to show the leadership style of coaching which is featured by less interpersonal behavior, more supportive behavior and more controlling behavior at the organizational development stage of mC.

Leadership Style of Decentralizing for the Development Stage of MC

For organizations at the development stage of MC, members have rich experiences, adequate skills and enough abilities to achieve goals and complete missions without the involvement of their leaders. Besides, members highly recognize and accept the instructions from leaders and are willing to execute tasks assigned by their leaders.

Leaders should reduce supportive behavior since organizational members have sufficient abilities and resources to accomplish missions independently. Leaders' supportive behaviors may be considered unnecessary and even useless. Excessive supportive behavior will probably result in a waste of leaders' time, energy and resources. Meanwhile, leaders should also reduce controlling behavior as organizations with both high levels of maturity and a high level of conformity can successfully accomplish expected goals without leaders' supervision or intervention. Excessive controlling behavior of leaders is not only unnecessary but is also easy to trigger resistance and distrust from employees.

Therefore, leaders should reduce both supportive behavior and controlling behavior at this development stage. Interpersonal behavior is what leaders should use most for organizations at the development stage of MC. It is suggested that leaders focus on maintaining good interpersonal relationships with employees and minimize their involvement in the daily operation and management of their organizations. In one word, leaders should choose to show the leadership style of decentralizing which is featured by fewer supportive behaviors, fewer controlling behaviors and more interpersonal behaviors at the organizational development stage of MC.

Leadership Style of Parenting for the Development Stage of Mc

Organizations at the development stage of Mc have a high level of maturity and low level of conformity. As organizational members have enough abilities and resources to complete missions independently, leaders can reduce their supportive behaviors of leadership.

Meanwhile, interpersonal behaviors should be frequently used by leaders to improve the mutual trust between leaders and employees and the level of organizational conformity. As members in organizations with a low level of conformity always refuse to accept commands from their leaders and often do what is prohibited by leaders, controlling behaviors should also be enhanced. In short, leaders should choose to show the leadership style of parenting which is featured by more controlling behaviors, more interpersonal behaviors and fewer supportive behaviors at the organizational development stage of Mc (see Table 12.4).

Jennifer, CEO of NOBE, used to believe that it was not necessary for her to involve deeply in the daily management and operation of her company as everything was on the right track. She praised the management philosophy of governing by non-interference. But gradually Jennifer found that the real situation was far from what she had expected. First of all, she was troubled by some veteran staff who were arrogant and defied the company's rules and regulations. These veterans always refused to obey the

TABLE 12.4

Leadership Styles for Four Stages of Organizational Development

Four Stages	Characteristics	Leadership Style	Behavioral Combination of Leadership Style
Development stage of mc	Low level of maturity low level of conformity	Partnering	More controlling behaviors More supportive behaviors More interpersonal behaviors
Development stage of mC	Low level of maturity high level of conformity	Coaching	More controlling behaviors More supportive behaviors Fewer interpersonal behaviors
Development stage of MC	High level of maturity high level of conformity	Decentralizing	More interpersonal behaviors Fewer controlling behaviors Fewer supportive behaviors
Development stage of Mc	High level of maturity low level of conformity	Parenting	More controlling behaviors More interpersonal behaviors Fewer supportive behaviors

instructions from their superiors and set very bad examples to young staff and newcomers. There were increasing conflicts between employees and their managers. Interpersonal harmony which used to be the corporate spirit of NOBE disappeared.

Second, Jennifer found that only a few of her team members were willing to assume responsibility and take accountability for consequences. Without her personal involvement, many problems couldn't be resolved and some important projects were unable to proceed as expected. Meanwhile, the previous working experience on which her staff relied heavily was no longer adequate enough to deal with new challenges.

Jennifer had to face the fact that the overall capability and competitiveness of her company had declined dramatically. It is obvious that Jennifer misjudged the development stage of her company. She took it for granted that NOBE had developed into the stage of MC (high level of maturity and high level of conformity). Therefore, she wished to employ the leadership style of decentralizing accordingly.

Actually, the organizational development of NOBE had not entered into the stage of MC but gradually slipped into the stage of mc (low level of maturity and low level of conformity). Therefore, Jennifer's leadership style of decentralizing did not fit with NOBE's development stage of mc, which inevitably led to conflicts, chaos and decrease in productivity. Jennifer

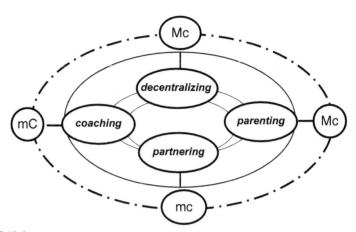

FIGURE 12.4
Leadership styles and organizational development stages.

should have switched her leadership style from decentralizing to partnering once she recognized correctly the real development stage of NOBE. More controlling behaviors, more supportive behaviors and more interpersonal behaviors should have been used by Jennifer in the short run to improve both maturity and conformity of her organization (Figure 12.4).

Conclusion—Learning and Practice of Gear-shifting Leadership

Followership, *face-to-face leadership*, *indirect leadership* and *organizational executive leadership*, as four independent and interdependent leadership gears, make up the complete system of gear-shifting leadership. Followership helps leaders win recognition and trust from both subordinates and superiors. The effectiveness of the other three gears is based on the successful practice of followership.

Face-to-face leadership enables leaders to better cultivate and develop direct subordinates and core team members. It is considered as a critical gear for leaders at all organizational levels. Indirect leadership shifts leaders' focus from managing individuals to managing teams. This leadership can exhibit leaders' influence and driving power on indirect subordinates as well as their abilities to improve the overall performance of teams. Organizational executive leadership enhances leaders' abilities to adapt to constant organizational changes through their dynamic optimizations.

There are four important principles that leaders are suggested to follow while they are learning and employing gear-shifting leadership, which are *comprehensive mastery of gear-shifting leadership*, *weakness improvement in gear-shifting leadership*, *prioritized enhancement in gear-shifting leadership* and *preparatory development of gear-shifting leadership*.

PRINCIPLE 1: COMPREHENSIVE MASTERY OF GEAR-SHIFTING LEADERSHIP

A common misunderstanding in learning and developing gear-shifting leadership is that leaders at higher organizational levels no longer need to learn and master lower levels of leadership gears. Leaders should realize that all the four gears are indispensable; and deficiency of any one of the four gears may cause the collapse of the overall leadership system. Even organizational executive leaders who are at the top of organizational pyramids should never overlook the significance of followership and face-to-face leadership.

Those who have defects in any of the four gears can't be considered as excellent leaders. Earlier in this book, the following incomprehensible phenomena in leadership were listed:

- *Why can't a charismatic leader with excellent self-management build an excellent team?*
- *Why can't a leader skilled in coaching team members adapt himself or herself to a revolutionary management environment?*
- *Why can't a leader good at strategic planning cultivate a core structure capable of sharing his or her own tasks?*
- *Why can't a leader with outstanding team management abilities be recognized and supported by his or her superiors?*
- *Why does a mid-level or grassroots manager regarded as an excellent future leader perform poorly in terms of leadership after being promoted to a higher position?*

Actually, all the above-mentioned phenomena reveal the same fact that leaders with excellent performance in some of the gears may be unqualified in others. Therefore, comprehensive mastery of gear-shifting leadership is a very important principle that leaders should follow. The four gears are all indispensable parts of the overall leadership system and leaders should never overemphasize one of them while overlooking others.

PRINCIPLE 2: WEAKNESS IMPROVEMENT IN GEAR-SHIFTING LEADERSHIP

To put gear-shifting leadership into practice, leaders also need to evaluate which one is their weakest gear and try best to repair that which may cause severe damage to the overall effectiveness of their own leadership. For leaders who perform well in face-to-face leadership, indirect leadership and organizational executive leadership, followership may be their biggest weakness if they cannot practice what they preach and set good examples to subordinates. These leaders should consider the improvement and repairment of followership as the first priority. Some leaders who are good at followership and face-to-face leadership may not be able to manage large-scale teams. Indirect leadership might be their weakest gear and should be improved immediately.

PRINCIPLE 3: PRIORITIZED ENHANCEMENT IN GEAR-SHIFTING LEADERSHIP

Job requirements of leaders at different organizational levels differ greatly. Leaders should place more emphasis on the development of leadership gears that match their own organizational ranks. For example, the gear that grassroots or front-line managers need to develop most is followership. These leaders who are working at low organizational levels drive and influence staff around them through giving full play to followership.

The most significant gear for mid-level managers may be face-to-face leadership, which focuses on developing and leading direct subordinates and core team members. Indirect leadership is the most significant gear for leaders of large-scale teams such as division directors or regional GM. These leaders need to improve their ability of indirect management in order to develop and control multi-level teams.

For the C-level leaders such as chairman, managing director, CEO, president and vice president, the gear in urgent need of development is organizational executive leadership. These leaders are responsible for dealing with organizational change and optimizing management modes dynamically.

PRINCIPLE 4: PREPARATORY DEVELOPMENT OF GEAR-SHIFTING LEADERSHIP

Once leaders get promoted to higher positions, leadership development should switch to a higher level of gears accordingly. Upgrade of leadership gears should keep pace with upgrade of leaders' organizational ranks. For example, if a leader who has been promoted to a C-level position is still relying heavily on his or her previous experience of face-to-face leadership, then the leadership development must have lagged behind job promotion.

Meanwhile, whatever ranks leaders are at currently and no matter whether they are to be promoted soon or not, learning and practicing of the leadership gear requested for higher positions should be done in advance. Simply, the upgrade of leadership gears should precede the upgrade of organizational ranks. To conclude, leaders at lower organizational levels can better prepare themselves for future promotion by developing higher-level leadership gears in advance.

Index

Note: Page numbers in *italics* indicate figures and in **bold** indicate tables on the corresponding pages.

Printed in the United States
By Bookmasters